University of Minnesota - Twin Cities
Department of Writing Studies

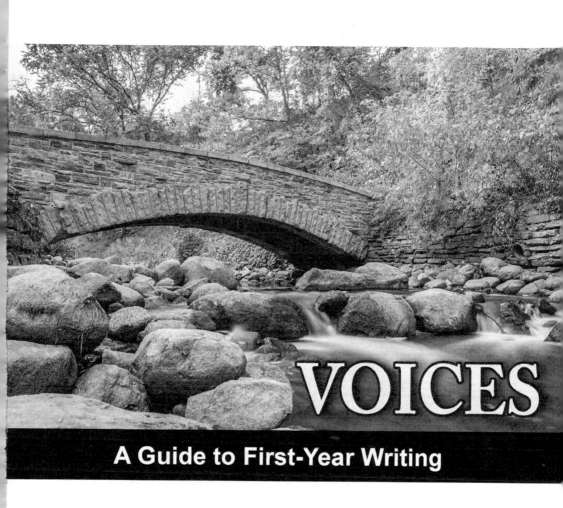

VOICES

A Guide to First-Year Writing

Third Edition

FOUNTAINHEAD
PRESS

Our green initiatives include:

Electronic Products and Samples. Products are delivered in non-paper form whenever possible via Xample, an electronic sampling system. Instructor samples are sent via a personalized web page that links to PDF downloads.

FSC-Certified Printers and Recycled Paper. All of our printers are certified by the Forest Service Council, which promotes environmentally and socially responsible management of the world's forests. This program allows consumer groups, individual consumers, and businesses to work together hand in hand to promote responsible use of the world's forests as a renewable and sustainable resource. Most of our products are printed on a minimum of 30 percent post-consumer waste recycled paper.

Cover and text design by: Lori Bryan

ISBN: 978-1-68036-721-8

Printed in the United States of America

Table of Contents

Acknowledgements

The purpose of the First-Year Writing (FYW) Handbook is to introduce instructors and students to the culture of writing and research at the University of Minnesota, highlight expectations, and provide resources for writing throughout the course and semester. The handbook was created to facilitate a shared, common experience and approach to the teaching, learning, and practice of writing within the FYW Program. The FYW Program appreciates the hard work of the many contributors who made this text possible.

Authors:
Patrick Bruch
Nicole Montana
Sarah Puett
Kate Peterson

Contributors:
Anne Fretheim
Sally Franson

Student Authors:
Brady Becker
Anaa Jibicho
Gayatri Lakshmi Narayanan
Daniel Picardo
Nathaniel Smith
Mateo Taddeini
Cody Tucholke
Xochitl Alejandra Villezcas

Authors' Notes

The FYW Program does not believe in decontextualized grammar instruction as a way to help students develop as writers. Studies show that grammar instruction outside of the context of students' own writing does not improve writing and rhetorical skills. You will encounter multiple and varied writing situations throughout your studies. This will require you to have a broader understanding of audience and a recognition of discipline-specific conventions. This doesn't mean that your instructor won't review grammar or conventions either in class or during individual conferences.

In order to provide a common, free source of information on grammar and conventions, the FYW Program worked with the U of M Libraries to publish *Supplemental Handbook Material for Voices*. This material, which is available online, is user-friendly, searchable, and can be downloaded in a variety of formats. http://open.lib.umn.edu/voiceshandbook/

Finally, it was the decision of the authors to utilize the plural pronoun of "they" or "them" when referring to singular subjects in this guide.

Part I

Welcome to the Conversation

Welcome to First-Year Writing (FYW) at the University of Minnesota! You are lucky because, while first-year writing is a common experience for almost every incoming freshman on almost every campus in the United States, your FYW Program is one of the few housed in a major research university. This means that the course you take will be informed by the latest research in Writing Studies about what writing is and how best to teach it. This handbook provides a guide to the experience you will have this semester. In this introductory piece, we offer an overview of the purpose, objectives, and approach to first-year writing that connects the many sections of FYW at the U of M.

Purpose

One of the key purposes of universities is to make new knowledge. The purpose of FYW is to provide an early opportunity for students to study and practice the main activities through which knowledge-making takes place: critical reading and writing that enables new contributions to ongoing conversations. Though every student has experiences with reading and writing, very few have truly engaged in reading and writing as **knowledge-making** activities. Transitioning and learning to approach writing in this new way is what makes first-year writing so important that it has been made a requirement. For you as a student, your writing class is an opportunity to spend a semester developing this essential activity through which your academic contributions will be channeled. It's a course about **your writing** and **your contributions** to broader conversations. In other words, your writing class, and your education as a whole, is an opportunity to add your ideas and insights to conversations regarding the topics you care about both as a student and as a citizen.

Objectives

Beyond the broad purpose of enabling new voices and views to join ongoing conversations, every section of first-year writing is guided by concrete objectives or learning outcomes. Specifically, you will explore diverse contexts and styles of reading and writing, develop a process of writing, and practice disciplines of research and study. These are described in more detail in the syllabus for your class and will be achieved over the course of the semester through each assignment. As you work to develop your writing and attain the learning objectives throughout the semester, you are gaining skills for active participation in making new knowledge.

Approach

Now that we've introduced the purpose and objectives of the class, let's discuss a little further the approach to writing that all sections share. When most people think about first-year writing, or "freshman comp" as it's sometimes known, they picture what might be called a "monological" approach to writing. In a monological approach, Writing (with a capital W) is imagined to be one thing in all times and places, and everyone in the classroom is expected to write and to be pretty much the same. Research has demonstrated that such approaches don't reflect the truth about writing, and they don't help students grow as writers. Instead, our program embraces a "dialogical" approach. Like a dialogue or conversation, our approach encourages students to recognize writing as an opportunity to **shape and be shaped**—to shape people's understandings of good writing at the same time that the conventions of academic writing shape you and your writing. Such an approach foregrounds the give and take of academic writing—that people's actions can and do inform, as they are informed by rules, conventions, and institutionalized expectations of what good writing looks like in particular times and places.

So what does this mean for the class you are taking in writing? It means that this class is not about a mythical **"One Right Way"** to write. Instead, it's about getting involved in writing as both a person who thinks about writing (and the work it does in various settings) and as a person who writes, who plans, who drafts, who reads and rereads, who revises, who shares and compares, who makes decisions, and who thinks and offers ideas. Writing, in this view, is an activity through which students can (and must) "take on" conventions in two senses—both *adopting* and *challenging* the forms of writing valued in the academy. Adopting conventions involves learning about them and making active choices to follow, to invest in and to be governed by some of the conventions you learn about. Challenging conventions means learning that conventions for good writing *constrain* writers as they enable writers to contribute their ideas. At times, your goals for your writing might justify resisting the usual or expected way of constructing your writing. These gestures of resistance can also broaden your audience's expectations of how good writing looks and sounds. For us, then, good writing is not writing that robotically echoes a mythical standard of perfection. Instead, good writing is writing that thoughtfully and effectively wrestles with ideas about topics and ideas about how to write about those topics.

Given this definition of good writing, it should not be a surprise that first-year writing classes emphasize writing that actively engages with other people's ideas and other people's writing. Thus, much, though not all, of the writing you'll be studying and practicing is writing that incorporates outside sources. This aspect of our approach goes back to our location in a knowledge-making institution. Knowledge-making doesn't happen in a vacuum. Instead, knowledge is made by **building on other people's work and ideas**. When you think about this notion of using your own writing to **build on others' ideas,** you can see how the "One Right Way" to write approach would never work. Instead of each of us saying the same thing in the same way, we need our writing to enable each of us to make our own unique additions (ideas) in our own ways (style). Your challenge this semester is to develop your abilities to make *your* contributions in *your* ways. In other words, to practice really writing. It's going to be a challenging and rewarding experience. Here we go!

Voices of Students

"Writing is a complex experience, not a series of steps."

Your FYW Course

The FYW Program at the U of M is housed in the Writing Studies Department. As such, the courses we run focus on the study and development of writing. Whether students are reading and writing about television shows, political campaigns, historical events, or fashion magazines, the central emphasis of every class is *writing*. Within this framework, reading about particular topics provides a chance to study how writing is being used by particular authors to present a particular version of the truth about a topic. The focus is not so much on the topic but exploring different strategic uses of writing to create a conversation around a topic. These conversations are influential because they profoundly shape how we see the world around us. As a student and as a citizen, you already participate in the conversations that create the world we all share. This course will help you do this more actively and provides an opportunity for you to develop skills and awareness in your writing that you'll use throughout your studies and for the rest of your life.

Our first-year writing courses are taught by professional writing instructors and graduate students from three departments: Writing Studies, English, and American Studies. This creates a community of instructors who are not only committed to the development of your writing but also who are representative of a broad variety of writing backgrounds and experiences. Your instructor will work with you throughout the semester as your guide to discovering where you are as a writer and where you can take your writing.

Course Design

Aside from this handbook, your instructor has devised their own version of the course that will introduce you to research and writing at the U of M. This means that your section and your experience are unique. Though one section might focus on the environment and another might focus on food, all sections share a focus on joining academic and public conversations through source-based writing. Your instructor has developed course content that reflects her or his expertise, and that will allow you to acquire the research, writing, and critical thinking skills needed for university-level writing. Over the course of the semester, you will write, revise, and get feedback on several shorter papers and a more elaborate researched paper. You will have a chance to work with classmates, to meet individually with your instructor, and to learn about writing resources on campus. By the end of the semester, you will have achieved the course learning objectives:

Develop a process of writing

- control pre-writing and planning strategies to arrive at a focused topic for a paper
- craft thesis statements that indicate a clear position on a topic and tie the paper together
- develop a topic through clearly structured paragraphs and the whole paper so that ideas are fully explained, assertions are backed up, supporting evidence is sufficient, and claims are credible
- through the sequence of assignments, develop a body of knowledge and growing perspective on a topic
- produce a researched paper that analyzes, synthesizes, and documents source material

Explore diverse contexts, resources, and choices in writing

- communicate their ideas and those of others to specific audiences
- write in appropriate academic genres and digital media to communicate with different audiences
- make choices in their own writing and articulate other options

Practice disciplines of research and study

- identify an author's audience, purpose, argument, and assumptions (i.e., critical reading) in an analysis paper or class discussion
- locate and evaluate relevant scholarly and popular sources on a research topic using library resources
- properly and ethically use MLA or APA documentation format for in-text and external bibliographic citations of scholarly, popular, and electronic sources

Office Hours

While you will meet at least once in conference with your instructor, your instructor holds office hours every week. These open hours are a good way to get answers to questions you may have, receive guidance on an assignment, resolve an issue you are having in class, or pick up materials you may have missed due to an absence. Students who visit their instructor during office hours often report how valuable the time is and how glad they are that they took advantage of the direct access to their instructor.

Although it can be helpful to let your instructor know you will be dropping by during their office hours, you should not hesitate to go because office hours are not scheduled appointments but rather are open hours. Instructors value office hours as well and will reschedule any that they need to miss. One question that sometimes arises is whether office hours can be used to make up for missed classes. While you can pick up missed handouts or assignments, instructors cannot "redo" class in office hours. Instead, you should get notes from peers and then follow up with the instructor with any specific questions. It is your responsibility to find out what you missed.

"My instructor gave us the independence to develop as writers while giving us the tools to advance our abilities."

One-on-one Conferences

At some point in the semester, your instructor will schedule a one-on-one conference with you. Each instructor utilizes conference time to accomplish a variety of different objectives, yet all will touch upon each student's progress. This is your best opportunity to receive direct feedback on your writing, and we encourage you to take advantage of the time you will have with your instructor. Prepare for the conference by completing any required activities you are to bring to your conference. If you will be discussing a particular piece of writing with your instructor, it would be beneficial for you to develop a list of questions you have about your draft. While your instructor will have a keen eye on your writing, determining what you want to ask your instructor before your meeting can also help you get the most out of your conferences.

Discussion

Whether your section is taught using a textbook, a book, or a collection of articles, your instructor has chosen the course readings based on what each piece can help you learn about writing. While instructors also choose readings for their content, you will read to discover the moves, techniques, and stylistic choices authors make in order convey meaning. Discussing and deconstructing how a text has been composed can help you think about your own writing. Understanding different writing techniques and ways to provide information will serve you throughout your studies.

Actively participating in class activities and discussion is vital to your experience in this course. In order to ensure everyone's access to a productive learning environment and intellectual freedom, everyone must remain respectful of each other's ideas. Your classroom community may have developed its own standards for discussion, and the U of M has a Code of Conduct that all students are expected to follow. If your section has an online discussion component, standards of discussion still apply. "Flaming" (posting offensive messages) or other hostile behaviors harm the learning environment. Though we are always free to disagree, all students are expected to contribute respectful comments to class discussions in each learning environment.

Voices of Students

"Discussions were interesting, fun, and stimulating. This was one of my favorite classes and it was *required* freshman writing."

Peer Review

Another important opportunity your first-year writing class will offer is the chance to participate in peer review. Though it takes many forms, peer review always involves reading and responding to your classmates' writing. The purposes of peer review fall into two big categories: learning to work with your own writing and learning to help others work with their writing. Let's think about each of these areas in a little more detail.

Learning to Develop Your Own Writing

One primary purpose of reviewing others' work in progress is to practice activities that you can apply to your own writing. These include learning to read with an eye toward the possibilities for even stronger presentation and development of a text's key messages. In fact, it's frequently only through drafting that we **discover** what it is that we are really trying to say in a piece of writing, and part of reading toward the possibilities of a draft is to focus on developing the point or central message of a text. Of course, there are times when a first draft is a final draft and half-baked ideas will serve just fine. But for those times when we want to present carefully constructed and thoroughly developed ideas that contribute as fully as possible to contexts in which we care about being taken seriously, drafting is essential. But saying this and accepting it to be true are not enough. What does it mean to work with and **develop** a draft? This is where peer review comes in. Through the peer review activities in your class, your instructor will provide you opportunities for guided practice in implementing strategies for working with drafts. As you work to use these strategies on peers' drafts, you are working to develop the same approaches that you can use to develop your own drafts.

Learning to Help Others Develop Their Writing

In addition to learning techniques for working with your own drafts, peer review is a chance to develop skill in helping others. This involves learning to be a "constructive critic." A constructive critic believes in the work that a text is trying to accomplish and seeks to identify strengths upon which further developments can be constructed. A delicate balance must be struck between supporting the author and taking over the paper. A central concept that will prove valuable here is that, as a reader, your job is to suggest possibilities and steps the author *could* take (rather than "should" take) to build further on what they have so far. It's very useful to hear about possible "next steps" and to discuss the possible effects of those suggestions even if only to spark other ideas that take the paper in other directions. In addition to helping your classmates think about how they want to develop their own drafts, learning to generate possibilities and the effects they would have on drafts is good for *your* work with your own writing.

Campus Resources

The U of M offers several academic support options that you can take advantage of outside of class to help advance your writing and research skills. You can choose to work on drafts with a consultant in the Center for Writing or seek assistance with your research with a peer research consultant in the library.

Center for Writing – Student Writing Support offers free face-to-face and/or online writing consultations with writing tutors to all U of M students in any stage of the writing process. You can visit the website for more information or to book an appointment: writing.umn.edu/sws.

Peer Research Consultants (PRC) and SMART Learning Commons – The U of M Libraries and the SMART Learning Commons offer peer tutoring and assisted learning, peer research consultations, and media production consultations. You can visit the website for more information on how to meet: www.lib.umn.edu/smart.

Student English Language Support (SELS) – The U of M offers free, face-to-face English as a Second Language Support to international undergraduate students through the Minnesota English Language Program. This support is designed for students who want to address a particular English language need, who have specific questions about learning English, or who need resources for polishing English skills. You can visit the website for more information on how to schedule an appointment: www.cce.umn.edu/minnesota-english-language-program/student-english-language-support.

Part II

The Writing Process

A word after a word after a word is power.
Margaret Atwood

As part of the U of M's first-year writing program, your instructor will guide you through a **process-oriented** approach to composition. Throughout the semester you will be encouraged to experiment and reflect on your writing process, and you'll develop your own strategies for each stage of the process so that your work can evolve.

Those new to writing sometimes think about the writing process as systematic and linear, much like methods used in scientific laboratories. With this kind of reasoning, writing a paper would work like this:

Prewriting
Brainstorming, sketching, freewriting, mapping, outlining

Writing
Drafting

Revising
Feedback, editing, proofreading

Yet as you have likely discovered through experience, the writing process is often less fixed than this model imagines. Instead, we often discover new thoughts as we are revising, and find that we need to go back into drafting and even brainstorming as we pursue new ideas. Part of what you'll be learning in this course is what approaches to the writing process are effective for you as you write and receive feedback on your work. Some writers may find they spend too much time on preliminary stages and have difficulties because they run out of time and wind up composing an entire draft the day before the due date. Other writers may find they are reluctant to revise their work after putting lots of time into the first draft. In this course, you'll learn to recognize your tendencies and see the writing process as something more circular and composed of overlapping elements.

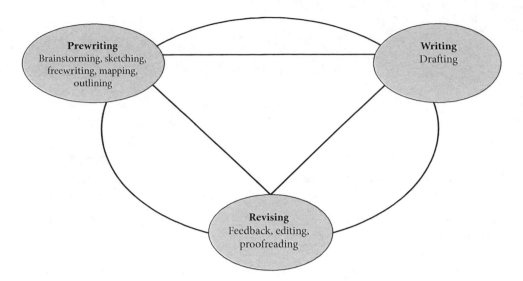

In what follows, we'll introduce some key concepts and stages of the writing process that your class will invite you to explore and experiment with.

Getting Started

The most difficult and complicated part of the writing process is the beginning.
A.B. Yehoshua

There are few experiences more anxiety-producing than staring at a blank document the night before a paper is due, knowing that over the course of those midnight hours, you somehow have to fill it. Sometimes this anxiety can lead students to do things that prove extremely harmful in the long run, like completely panicking and plagiarizing a paper. Here in FYW, we know that no student enters a course with the intent to plagiarize; rather, these things happen when the process becomes overwhelming and students feel they have run out of options. Research shows that writers get ready for the task of writing by separating big things (a whole paper) into smaller things (a list of possible examples to discuss). Your class will be organized around activities to help you and your peers work together to build your essays over time.

While many students have received extensive instruction on writing, few have been encouraged to identify and develop the most effective **prewriting strategies** for their individual writing process. This course will assist you in articulating what you already know is successful in your process so that you can also determine how you want to further develop your process. If you're thinking, "But I don't have a process!" chances are you do—you just haven't articulated it yet. By reflecting on the process, you begin to take control over your process and your writing. The ability to sit down and write ceases to be a mystical phenomenon, something that some people "just have" and others never will, and becomes a set of practical activities for thinking, creating, and discovering—building the smaller pieces that larger texts are made of.

Whatever your process becomes, you may find it useful to think about "getting started" as the stage in which you say *yes*. New ideas are allowed; tangents are encouraged. You are a creator in this stage, not a critic. Early on, the idea is to trust the process and let the activities of drafting lead you to places, ideas, connections, and insights that you wouldn't otherwise have discovered.

Voices of Students

"The writing process isn't a concrete set of guidelines. You can adjust it to something that works best for you."

Drafting

Almost all good writing starts with terrible first efforts.
Anne Lamott

Essayist Anne Lamott's thought that our first efforts will be terrible may be difficult to accept, but the upside is in the rest of her sentence—none of us are alone in leaving the early stages of the process with something inadequate that *can be good*. And really, our early work isn't terrible *as a first effort*, it's only terrible *as a final draft*.

Many of you are familiar with the process of turning "rough drafts" in to your writing instructor for feedback before composing a "final draft." Your FYW class is about helping you learn to work with drafts so that you have plenty of time and space to improve your ideas and writing before the final draft is due. Instead of thinking of the drafting process as writing one "terrible" and one "finished" draft, you may create a number of drafts to allow your ideas to fully develop. In a way, drafting never really ends, as each of your drafts moves you closer to realizing your contribution to the conversation.

Feedback

Feedback from your instructor will not address every aspect of your writing. Instead, effective writing teachers help students identify and pursue next steps for building on strengths that stand out in their writing. This positive approach to fostering growth means that the feedback you get on one assignment is not the only aspect of your writing to work on. Throughout the semester, you will also receive a good amount of verbal and written feedback from your peers. It's especially useful to get feedback from someone who knows the assignment, the context, and the language of your course. Aside from your instructor and your classmates, you may also find it useful to ask a roommate or another friend to look at your writing. Seeking out feedback from a variety of sources is especially important to the development of your writing and your process.

Voices of Students

"My instructor provided me with great feedback on every paper, both written and in person, and truly helped me to become a better writer. I feel like I have grown as a person."

Revision

Many students in FYW courses struggle with "what comes next" after completing a first draft of a paper or assignment. Revision, as it's taught currently in secondary schools, is often confused with proofreading—that is, a grammar-based approach to improving sentences in drafts with little to no attention paid to the ideas you are trying to share and your evolving sense of how your ideas relate to other writers' ideas. Yet the real purpose of revision is present in the word itself: a revision of what a piece of writing can or will be. In order to truly revise our work then, we have to abandon our preconceived notions of what the work is, so that we can approach it *as if for the first time*. Often, this means letting go of what has already been written and our attachments to it (the time we already put in! that great sentence we wrote at two in the morning!) in order to explore and express our ideas better. Think of yourself as a sculptor with a giant block of marble in front of you. Little by little, you chip away with your tools until a shape begins to arise. First the outline emerges, then something with more detail. Take Michelangelo's *David*, for example.

What might have happened if Michelangelo had put down his chisel after making a rough version of a man out of marble and thought to himself, "Eh, that's basically what I had in mind"? Perhaps it would have looked something like this:

The reason that proofreading is often an ineffective method of revision is that it encourages you to set the fine details of your paper in stone before it's time to do so. Revision, as it's taught in the FYW Program, is meant to help you rethink, clarify, concentrate, and convey your ideas so that you may eventually perform the task of polishing sentences and turning in a finished draft. True revision is hard work, but you may find that your best ideas emerge in the writing between your first and final drafts.

Writing is rewriting. Writing is recursive. We return to our writing, over and over again, so that we can mean what we say and say what we mean using the most precise language possible.

"I thought the writing process was linear, now I see it as cyclic."

Voices of Students

Strategies for Revision

In the timeline of writing a paper, there are many different points at which you may revise. Depending on your writing process, you'll find and develop different strategies that work for you. Below are two strategies you can use at any time.

Whether or not you've gotten feedback, and have read over the comments on your draft, it's best to take a day or two to think about suggested revisions, changes you want to make, and new ideas to include before beginning.

Reverse Outlines

Typically, we think of doing an outline before you write a paper. Reverse outlining, however, is done after you've written the paper and will allow you to recognize problems with your claim, your evidence, and your organization. This technique is helpful because we don't always think about these issues while we're furiously writing a draft. Here's how to do it.

First, write out your claim. Then, read through your essay and write the main idea or ideas of each paragraph. You're creating a list of what each paragraph is about, without worrying too much about your reasoning. The trick is to be honest. You might've meant for each paragraph to have a strong main idea, but if it's not there, that's ok. That's revision! Use this template for your reverse outline:

Claim:
Para 1:
Para 2:
Para 3:
Para 4:
Para 5:
Para 6:
Para 7:
Para 8:

Remember, good paragraphs have a topic sentence that expresses one main idea, an example that shows that idea, and an explanation for the reader. After finishing the template above, consider the following questions:

- Which of my paragraphs has more than one main idea?
- Which of my paragraphs doesn't seem to have a strong main idea at all?
- Does each paragraph support my claim?
- Does each paragraph build on the next in a logical way?

After doing the reverse outline, decide how to revise the content and order of your paragraphs. Do this with a peer if you can. You might also find that you can change or shift the wording of your claim based on what your paragraphs show.

Revision Checklist

Before beginning to take your paper through the checklist, read your paper aloud to see if there are any points at which you ramble, stumble, or lose interest. Mark those areas for review.

Purpose
- ❑ Is your introduction engaging? Does it inform the reader of why they should continue reading?
- ❑ Is your claim clear, strong, and specific to the task?

Organization
- ❏ Is your evidence arranged effectively? Does one idea lead into the next?
- ❏ Are paragraphs the appropriate length? Do you discuss more than one idea per paragraph?
- ❏ Can you sharpen your topic sentences?
- ❏ Are you missing transitional words or sentences?

Content
- ❏ Are the main ideas given enough weight? Are there any ideas that need to be discussed further?
- ❏ Have all claims been adequately supported and discussed? Should you do more research?
- ❏ Is all supporting material relevant to the discussion?
- ❏ Are any logical fallacies present?
- ❏ Is your reasoning deliberate, controlled, convincing?
- ❏ Are quotations and visual material (pictures, charts, tables, etc.) introduced before they are presented or explained after?

Clarity
- ❏ Do you have a variety of sentence styles?
- ❏ Does every sentence have a purpose in your paper? Can you cut any extraneous text?
- ❏ Is your word choice appropriate for the topic and audience?
- ❏ Does your paper present a consistent tone and focus throughout?
- ❏ Are there any shifts in tense or point of view (I, we, he, she, it, they, etc.)?

Format
- ❏ Have you titled your paper?
- ❏ Are headings and subheadings, if used, set correctly?
- ❏ Are sources and evidence properly credited and documented?
- ❏ Do citations follow the necessary style throughout (MLA, APA, etc.)?

Developing Rhetorical Awareness

Reading is an essential component to every section in the U of M's FYW program. Regardless of what topics your instructor has chosen, each reading has been selected as an example of writing that utilizes specific techniques and strategies to convey information or make an argument. By exploring the choices each writer makes, you will be able to see how each text is deliberately constructed. This practice will help you when it is time for you to make choices in your own writing.

Yet what about the meaning that is made through deliberate choices? Each writer has a purpose and reason for presenting information and for choosing specific evidence from their research to support or illuminate their claims. When we encounter a text, we must approach each reading critically. **Critical reading** helps us determine how we understand the overall point of the text, how each part relates to the overall point, and how we assess its overall validity. By critically analyzing a text, we can determine *why* it matters and what it adds to the larger conversation on a topic. Without such analysis, we may be persuaded to believe only one version of the truth, which is really only **one** side of the story.

Critical reading means you will actively:

- Evaluate the writer's credibility and potential biases
- Analyze the argument the writer makes
- Determine the argument's validity through analyzing evidence
- Discover the argument's limitations, if any
- Decide where the writer's viewpoint fits in the larger conversation on the topic

By now, you may have developed reading strategies that help you determine the main ideas of a text. You might utilize pre-reading strategies such as previewing a text or generating pre-reading questions. You also might use reading practices such as marking up a text, making notes in the margins, highlighting, or mapping out main ideas. These strategies and practices allow you to engage with a text. In this way, you are no longer a passive reader but an active reader, determining the content of a text.

Throughout the semester, you will encounter a variety of texts that will challenge you to decipher how meaning is made and communicated through different writing situations. Across the University, different disciplines use various forms of essays or writing situations to communicate information with their peers and students. For example, the structure and delivery of content in a lab report differs greatly from a literary analysis. Developing and enhancing your writing abilities in this course will allow you to successfully move through each writing situation you encounter throughout your academic career. How one approaches a particular writing situation depends on **the rhetorical situation**. The rhetorical situation consists of determining who the author is, the purpose of the piece, the topic, the intended audience, and the context/culture the piece is situated in. Likewise, active reading should begin by determining

The Rhetorical Situation

We communicate in a variety of ways every day. Whether we're texting, emailing, tweeting, posting, or writing, we're creating content that is being shared with others. In each method of communicating, we alter the way in which we share information. For example, you wouldn't write a thank-you card to a grandmother in the same way you'd text a friend about plans for the weekend. Your grandmother probably would not understand the abbreviated language and slang you use. Each method of communication and intended recipient is unique, and this changes the way you write. These elements are part of what we call the rhetorical situation.

There are five elements to each rhetorical situation:

- Author – The individual who creates the communication
- Audience – Those who receive the communication (e.g., peers, instructors, friends)
- Purpose/Goal – The reason for the communication (e.g., to report information)
- Text/Medium – The actual instance or form of communication
- Setting – The context of the communication (e.g., time, place, culture, environment)

So why is it important to understand and know the rhetorical situation of each text you develop as a writer or encounter in your research?

How to Apply Rhetorical Situation to Your Writing

When you are the author of a piece, knowing who your audience is will allow you to create an appropriate piece of writing that communicates necessary information in a way that the intended audience can understand.

Next, knowing what you hope to achieve—your ultimate goal or purpose—will allow you to make deliberate choices in your writing that effectively convey your message.

Choosing the appropriate method of communication, whether you make a video, create a presentation or write a paper, for your message can impact the way it is received.

Finally, understanding the setting or context surrounding your message is important when determining what influence your message can have on its audience. Is the information relevant to the time and place of its delivery? How is your message informed by the cultural, societal, and/or political climate it is a product of? How does your message contribute to or disrupt the environment or community it interacts with?

How to Apply Rhetorical Situation to Texts You Encounter

- Know the stance and/or intent of the author.
- Determine who the piece is for and examine how this affects how the message is conveyed.
- Know the setting in order to examine how it interacts with the message.
- Consider limitations or benefits of the medium of the message.

the rhetorical situation of the text or other form of media you are studying. This course, and many you will encounter throughout your studies, will include writing assignments that ask you to synthesize the ideas you have read and develop your own thoughts to add to the conversation around a topic. To do this, you will read source material and complete research not to prove a thesis right or wrong, but to provide ideas that lead you to discover some truth, support your claim and lead you to develop your own idea. When we actively engage with a text, we can begin to also identify one's assumptions and investigate the validity of those assumptions. If we approach a reading or an idea assuming we know how it impacts or detracts from our own ideas, we may never move forward along the line of critical thinking to informed action. For example, if we assume that a cause has only one effect our ability to discover other potential outcomes may be limited. Identifying our own assumptions also allows us to see how our own realities have been created. If we encounter an idea that is in direct opposition to our version of the truth, as critical readers, we will investigate the validity of the argument or reasoning that developed the idea. However, we must also take time to uncover how we formulated our own assumptions by identifying our beliefs about the world around us. What is a **fact**? What is **opinion**? What **evidence** are we using to support our own **claims**? Building a solid argument based on carefully constructed lines of thought that are supported by sound evidence cannot happen unless we have insight into our own ideas and intentions.

Claim, Opinion, Fact

As a genre, academic writing consists of a variety of writing situations and styles. The papers you will write will ask you to complete some form of action with some form of material, and most writing situations you encounter will ask you to make some form of a claim or take a position. In general, claims and positions must be arguable and based on verifiable information such as facts. Here are some ways to determine if you have an arguable claim and facts or if you're simply offering your opinion.

Claim: A claim is a statement or position that is arguable and can be supported by evidence such as statistics, expert testimony, research results, facts, and more. A claim is not based on one's own opinion. Instead, a claim is developed by examining information and making an assertion.

Opinion: An opinion is one's personal belief or view about something. An opinion is subjective because it is based on personal experience or preference. Opinions can be supported by facts, but that does not make an opinion a fact or a claim. When someone uses their opinion to make a claim, they are really making an argument based on what they personally believe to be facts. To formulate a claim from an opinion, a writer must determine what logical, objective information they have concerning the topic and what is fact versus personal experience.

Fact: A fact is a piece of information that can be verified or proven to have occurred or be true. A fact can be used as evidence to support a claim. While a fact is thought to be indisputable or undeniable, facts *can* change especially over time when new information is discovered. It is important to complete your research using the most current information available.

In order to understand what an author says, along with the rhetorical situation, you will need to have an understanding of how arguments are made and recognize both the strategies and the **logical fallacies** that can occur in each text you encounter. This will require you to also understand the **rhetorical concept** the author is using to appeal to the reader.

Rhetorical Concepts

Writers use rhetorical strategies in crafting and delivering their points of view on a topic in a piece of writing. Below is a list of four common rhetorical concepts used to appeal to an audience. A writer specifically chooses a concept to use based on the writing situation and topic of discussion.

Ethos – When writers use ethos, they rely on their own or an expert's credibility or character to appeal to the audience. The writer aims to gain an audience's trust.

Pathos – A writer uses pathos to connect to their audience through appealing to the audience's emotions. Attention is paid to the values and beliefs of the audience. Writers may craft "what if" scenarios that audience members can relate to in order to persuade them to take action.

Logos – When a writer uses logos, the result is writing that uses logic or reason to appeal to an audience. An argument built using logos is usually clear, well-organized, and supported by research and data.

Kairos – When a writer publishes a piece, delivers a speech, or sends a message at the "right time," kairos is being used. Further, the word choice and tone of the writing is appropriate for the audience at the time.

In this course you will learn the differences between the various types of texts that you will use as sources for your research. You will identify what a *good* source is through actively evaluating each text or media you find on your topic. Spending time analyzing a web page or looking into an author's potential bias will help you find information that is relevant to your studies and determine not only the validity of the information, but also if the source's contribution to the conversation is important. A critical reader will ask: does this source move the conversation forward, and how does it fit within the larger discussion?

Common Logical Fallacies

- *Ad hominem* - This fallacy attacks a person's character rather than addressing the matter at hand.
- *Appeal to Authority* - This fallacy occurs when an authority or expert makes a claim that is outside their expertise and it is accepted as true without proper support.
- *Appeal to Ignorance* - This fallacy occurs when an author maintains their claim must be true due to a lack of evidence to the contrary. The author effectively makes it the responsibility of the audience to provide such evidence.
- *Bandwagon Appeals* - This fallacy maintains that because others do something or think a certain way, we should all do or believe the same.
- *Either/or* - This fallacy promotes the idea that there can only be two possible positions on a complex issue.
- *Faulty Causality* - This fallacy makes the assumption that if one event follows another, the first event must have caused the second.
- *Hasty Generalizations* - A faulty conclusion about a studied population is made if it is based on insufficient data or unqualified evidence in a study.
- *Red Herring* - A red herring fallacy distracts and diverts attention to an issue having little to no relevance to the real issue.
- *Slippery Slope* - A slippery slope argument assumes that one event will automatically lead to another without any evidence that such a cause and effect will take place.
- *Status Quo* - This fallacy maintains the "status quo" and promotes the idea that if things are a certain way, they should stay that way. As well, if something is not occurring, this fallacy maintains it should continue not to occur.
- *Two Wrongs* - This fallacy occurs when an author justifies a stance or action because someone else believes or behaves in a certain way. This line of thinking posits that "two wrongs make a right."

Voices of Students

"You won't be able to tune out in class, hand in papers, and get a good grade. You have to be active and show that your writing is active also."

Writing Arguments

There are several different approaches to argumentation that can be helpful to your writing. The goal of informal logic and argumentation is to create a claim supported by evidence. The following material can help you plan, write, and revise the logic of your papers.

The two basic ways we create arguments are through inductive and deductive reasoning. **Inductive reasoning** uses specific, representative cases and creates a generalization. For example, "First-year writing is required at the University of Minnesota so all universities must require first-year writing." **Deductive reasoning** uses a generalized statement and applies it to a specific case. For example, "First-year writing is required for all University of Minnesota students, and I am a University of Minnesota student, so I am required to take first-year writing."

Toulmin Argument Structure allows you to create and examine the working parts of an argument: data, warrant, claim. A **claim** is what you want to establish. The **data**, or grounds, are the explicit reasons you give. The **warrant** is the evidence or guarantee that connects the data to the claim. Though you might have one major claim for your paper, you might have several data and warrants that make up your paragraphs. Here is a simplified visual of Toulminian structure with an example below.

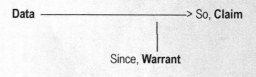

Data ————————————————————> So, **Claim**

Since, **Warrant**

Data 1 ——————————————————> So, **Claim**
Damaging earthquakes   Buying a home in southern
frequently occur in this area.   California is unwise.

Since, **Warrant 1**
Scientists note a high frequency of plate movement in
this area.

Data 2 ——————————————————> So, **Claim**
Homes in this area are   Buying a home in southern
prohibitively expensive.   California is unwise.

Since, **Warrant 2**
Real estate aggregates show average home prices
above $1 million in this area.

Part III

Research and Writing

I write entirely to find out what I'm thinking, what I'm looking at, what I see and what it means. What I want and what I fear.
Joan Didion

It's a common falsehood that writers know exactly what they're going to say when they begin; that when a writer sits down, there's some bright, guiding light directing them from within. In reality, we often have no idea what we're going to say. We don't know what to say, and we definitely don't know how to say it in the beginning. We only know that we want to say *something*, and we want other people to connect with our writing. In this way, writing is part of a shared social experience. We often read the work of others in order to find our own arguments, our own selves, somewhere in the mix. There's a give and take involved in writing, both with ourselves and with the ideas of others.

As part of your FYW experience at the U of M, you have the opportunity to research, write, research some more, and write again. Research can take many forms, many of which are already a part of your daily life (e.g., which bus do I need to take to get to East Bank?). A research-driven writing process includes talking with your peers, reading the work of others, and writing reflectively about a given topic. Your questions and ideas about your topic will grow and shift over time. Time, it turns out, is actually an important part of the research process. Your instructor will have different types of assignments built in as part of the research paper, but allowing your thoughts to develop over time can be incredibly helpful.

I write because I don't know what I think until I read what I say.
Flannery O'Connor

In a given research project, you might get to choose your own topic or your instructor may assign you one. But it's important that you care, to some degree, about what you're going to research and write about. Choosing a topic can be a challenge for writers, but there are plenty of ways to start. You might begin with the works you've read in class, or any of the other reading that you do, as a source of ideas. You might only be interested in one part or idea from a text, but you can ask yourself things like, why does this happen? What assumptions are made here? What's the association between this and something else? What about this am I passionate about telling others? Where do I see this taking place in my own life? Give yourself time to notice arguments that are present in your life, which might lead you to a topic you can make new knowledge about.

Mind Map

A mind map or bubble map is a type of thinking map that helps you to generate ideas, topics, and subtopics. These maps can also help to organize, to see relationships between ideas, and to see what might be missing. Start by putting a topic idea in the center. Quickly (e.g., 5 minutes) write down other topics, subtopics, names, places, events, dates, questions, keywords, synonyms, etc. This can help at different times in the research writing process, for example, at the beginning when you are just trying to think of an idea or when you are figuring out how to organize or outline your writing.

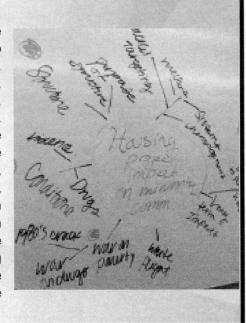

Fill in the mind map below.

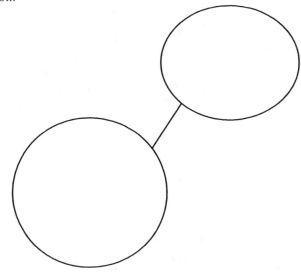

Once you find something interesting to read and write about, you might find that everything you read feels related to your topic. You could reasonably read about a topic for the entire semester and still not learn everything there is to know. Remember that the goal is for you to say *something* about your topic, with and alongside the voices of others. At some point you have to stop reading and start writing. It can be tempting to simply present information to your readers, to say, "Look at all of this! Isn't it interesting? Can you believe it?" But the goal is to add your unique voice to the conversation that others are taking part in. Taking time to think and using different opportunities to write about your topic will help you generate that contribution.

Bibliographies and Annotated Bibliographies

"Bibliography" is a broad term used to describe the list of sources that are referred to in a source-based publication. For the purposes of your FYW class, you'll likely use MLA or APA citation style to organize your bibliographies, which are also called "Works Cited" and "References" pages, respectively. Both of these serve the purpose of documenting what source material contributes to the work that precedes it. Examples of MLA and APA citations are provided in this handbook.

A unique type of bibliography is the annotated bibliography. Annotated bibliographies are used during the research process to help you keep track of your sources and use them effectively in the final paper. For each source, you'll organize, summarize and evaluate the material you've collected as you researched your topic. As with a regular bibliography, you'll include a citation for each source, followed by a short paragraph that describes the work, called an annotation. Below is an example from an APA annotated bibliography on the topic of welfare.

SUMMARY: In this article, Ehrenreich discusses welfare assistance in America as it applies to single parents, as well as how minimum wage affects these households. She argues against the idea that putting single mothers on welfare increases the likelihood that they will keep having children they cannot take care of. **DATA**: She uses statistics to show that most people who go on welfare are hardworking individuals who just do not make enough on their own to support themselves, much less their children. **PLAN**: This article will help me show that while the government does offer assistance to single parents, it does not offer enough, and it offers assistance in a way that makes the general public scoff at and belittle those who accept it. **SPECIFICS**: This also will help me highlight what individuals who received welfare really do with the money **RHETORICAL AWARENESS**: to build the credibility of hardworking single parents who do not abuse the system.

In writing annotations, you'll determine the source's claim and what its significance is in relation to your project. The form these annotations take might look different depending on your instructor. For example, you might write annotations about the methods, findings, or arguments of a given work, or you might write annotations that indicate a source's reliability or specific application to your research paper. In any case, these annotations are incredibly useful ways to see how your sources fit together (or don't). Writing these annotations will prepare you to synthesize the sources into a research paper that is uniquely informed by your reading of the material.

Of course, conversations we have (or read) and things that occur in the world constantly reshape how we feel. For example, you might read a satirical piece about giving all your money to those in need, like "The Singer Solution to World Poverty," and find it ridiculous. But then something happens. An earthquake devastates southern Asia, or a hurricane ravages the southern region of the United States, and suddenly your feelings about charity are reshaped by those events. We are constantly reshaped by the things that happen around us. Through your writing, you too have the opportunity to reshape the thoughts of others. It's both a responsibility and a delight to have that kind of influence.

Acknowledging the Contributions of Others

All writers struggle to find the right words. In some cases, we search every corner of our brains or hearts and sometimes we still can't get any words on the page. This feeling of fear and paralysis can be especially nerve-racking when you have a draft due the next morning for peer review. In other cases, we come across a text that perfectly says what we feel like we want to say, and they've captured it so well. We think, "Well they've said it better than I could." When you find yourself in this situation, in daily life or with respect to a writing assignment, you might feel like you have nothing to add to the conversation or that there's no room for your own thoughts.

Voices of Students

"I don't stress out about plagiarism anymore. Now I concern myself with giving credit where credit is due."

Feeling stuck is a completely normal part of the writing process. It is a deeply introspective task you're being asked to do. Figuring out how you think about a topic and putting those thoughts on paper can be difficult, but it can also be deeply rewarding. FYW is about acknowledging the challenges of writing and finding approaches that help you to build your drafts. The goal is to explore the way that you write and what you think needs to be written. All writers deserve to be acknowledged for their unique ideas and contributions. Naturally, part of the research process includes reading and writing about the work of others. Our understanding of what we read helps shape our understanding of a topic or situation. How could it not? Building on the work of others is how progress is made, ideas are expanded, and new knowledge is created. We rely on others to help us build our arguments, theories, or expressions, and thus we give credit where credit is due. In fact, acknowledging how the work of others helps us form our own ideas is fulfilling because it affirms our membership in the community and its conversations. It's like tracing your steps to show someone else the way: we show others how we got to where we are so they can follow us and build further on our ideas.

Voices of Students

"...how important it is to think freely while writing, how important it is to challenge common types of writing, and how important it is to explore your own style of writing throughout this course."

How do we do this? How do we trace our steps and still find our own way? Your instructor will discuss documentation practices with you in class, and there are examples of current MLA and APA style on page 51 of this handbook. These discussions of MLA, APA, or other documentation styles will help you ethically incorporate the work of others in your own writing. But there are some practical ways to avoid situations where you feel stuck and tempted to use someone else's work as your own. Whether you're in this situation, or if you just don't know what's considered plagiarism and what isn't, these strategies will help you be successful in your research process.

❚ Start Early

Begin thinking about your research topic as soon as your instructor mentions it in class. The sooner you can start reading and talking with someone about your topic, the better prepared you will be when it comes time to find sources and write. One of the best ways to organize your thoughts is to keep a research journal that tracks your thoughts, feelings, discoveries, or questions about a topic. Even if you're just scribbling down some notes, this will help you trace your own steps.

❚ Organize Your Sources

As you begin reading and finding information about a topic or topics, make note of where or how you read something. If you read a certain quote or section that really hits home with you, copy and paste or rewrite it with the citation information. Your instructor will suggest a particular citation style, such as MLA or APA, so use those requirements as a guide. Write down all the bibliographic details for each source. This information will be used on your Works Cited or References page. You will also need this information for in-text citations. Annotated bibliographies, literature reviews, or other preparatory assignments will also help you get organization.

Understand Common Knowledge

Knowing when to cite information can be tricky. How do you decide what needs to be cited and what doesn't? As a general rule, it's better to have cited and not needed to than not to have cited at all. Sometimes though, certain cultural information probably doesn't need to be cited, like who was president in 1960. Even though you might have needed to look this up, either online or in an encyclopedia, you wouldn't be expected to cite your source. But if you are discussing a specific opinion about who was president in 1960, about their policymaking for instance, that information would require a citation. Common knowledge can be a complicated issue and often varies according to your audience, so ask your instructor if you're unsure.

Use Your Resources

As a student at the U of M, you have access to an unprecedented number of resources. The librarians, peer research consultants, writing center staff members, and your instructor are all available to help you work on your writing. Take advantage of these resources, especially when you're having trouble finding your own words or blending your own voice with someone else's.

Keep in mind that your writing is an extension of yourself. We all want to be acknowledged for the things we've written because it's so intimately connected to who we are. Your writing is a unique and valuable addition to the university and to society, and plagiarizing won't help you make that contribution. Sometimes you may need further clarification on whether or not you're ethically handling your source material. For more information, see Part IV: Documentation Style Guides.

Synthesizing Sources

Putting your sources in conversation with one another is central to the research project. You're tasked with showing the reader how the ideas from your sources fit together to form a coherent argument of your own. It's important to remember that while the connections may be clear to you, your reader requires an explanation of what the source is, why it's relevant, and what it means in relation to your argument. This means that you should introduce and situate the source, as well as discuss and apply it. Don't expect your sources to speak for themselves. No matter if it's a paraphrased, summarized, or a quoted passage, you want to answer the "so what?" question for your reader. Frequently authors try to balance among the different ways to integrate sources into their writing.

Paraphrase

A paraphrase is a restatement, in your own words, of a passage from a source. You can use a paraphrase to integrate your source information into your work without seeming like you are simply relying on the words of your sources to illustrate or support your points. Because paraphrases contain ideas that are not your own, they need to be cited properly. Whether you're using MLA or APA style, there are specific criteria for documenting your sources. Please refer to the appropriate documentation section for more information.

Summary

Summaries can be a useful tool to research writers because they allow writers to use entire books and large documents by condensing information into smaller, more manageable pieces. It is common for research writers to summarize entire works, sometimes using only a single sentence. In some cases, a summary might occupy one or more paragraphs or be integrated into the discussion contained in one or more paragraphs. You can also use summaries to convey key information or ideas from a source without summarizing the entire source. You can summarize an entire source, or specific ideas and information from a source or a group of sources.

Quotation

Quotes can be used to introduce an idea, to support or clarify a point or term, or to illustrate positions on an issue. You should use direct quotations when you want to use an author's or expert's exact words, the exact words of someone who has firsthand experience with the issue you are researching, a passage in a source that features an idea you want to argue for or against, or a passage in a source that provides a clear and concise statement that would enhance your project document. Quotations can be parts of sentences (partial), whole sentences (complete), or long passages (block), all of which require a particular in-text citation. When quoting a source, try to consider what the author's quote does for your paper. Below is a list of sample signal verbs that you could use in place of something neutral, such as "Johnson says..." Be sure to think critically about what the author says and what the source does for your paper in choosing a signal verb.

Sample Signal Verbs

acknowledges, adds, admits, affirms, agrees, argues, asserts, believes, claims, comments, compares, confirms, contends, declares, demonstrates, denies, disputes, emphasizes, endorses, grants, illustrates, implies, insists, notes, observes, points out, reasons, refutes, rejects, reports, responds, states, suggests, thinks, underlines, writes

Research at the U of M

As earlier chapters have discussed, first-year writing involves thinking in new ways, writing as a representation of your thinking, and using the work of others to develop your ideas. As mentioned earlier, we often read the work of others in order to find our own arguments, our own selves, somewhere in the mix. This chapter explores strategies to help you discover and organize sources for your writing.

You are already an expert at finding information—using Google or Wikipedia to learn more about a topic, using Facebook or Twitter to find out about a friend, using a news site to find out about a breaking story. FYW will introduce you to an expanded way of gathering information. While it might not seem so, the initial results of a Google or Wikipedia search are extremely limited. Frequently the loudest voices drown out others' views. This makes Google a great tool to find out how late your favorite coffee shop is open but not as great for doing academic research. The University Libraries and the website (http://www.lib.umn.edu) provide access to a wider range of sources, including books, journals, data, music, and videos.

Getting Started with Academic Research

Research is about listening to and joining an ongoing conversation by finding, reading, and reacting to diverse sources. Thus, each new project can feel like getting to know a new neighborhood. It requires patience to spend time on something that might not feel efficient, and it takes persistence to work through those feelings of uncertainty and push through to completion. It also requires an open mind to find and wrestle with differing viewpoints and figure out your stance.

The first step in undertaking library research is defining your topic. A well-defined topic or research question will allow you to search with specific keywords and find useful sources instead of finding thousands of results that are only loosely related to your topic.

Keywords and Search Terms

A good way to get started thinking about your topic or research question is to explore the conversation that currently exists. Look up your topic idea in Google, Wikipedia, or other online encyclopedias. Read and skim to get background information on your topic including associated vocabulary, jargon, and key terms. Write down words and keywords on your topic in the boxes below, such as significant figures in the conversation, central issues, ideas, and points of debate. Select the words that most clearly capture your interest or angle on the conversation as it currently exists. Try to think of alternative words that authors might use, such as "adolescent" rather than "teen."

Libraries Search Tools and Databases

The University Libraries have a variety of tools that search and find academic journals, magazines, books, and more on your topic. The library catalog, **MNCAT Discovery**, searches through the physical items in our collection like books, DVDs, maps, artifacts, etc. It also searches through millions of online journal articles, books, magazines, and newspaper articles.

Another way to search is directly through the specialized databases of journals and magazine articles on specific subjects. For example, a database like "Business Source Premier" searches business journals, business magazines, and business newspapers. A database like "PsycINFO" searches psychology journals, psychology magazines, and psychology newspapers. We also have databases that search a specific type of collection. For example, "ARTstor" searches art images, and the "New York Times Proquest Historical Newspapers" Archive searches all pages since the paper began in 1851.

Just like writing, the research process is recursive. As you begin to review sources that you find in databases, you will sharpen your sense of who else is doing research and writing about this topic. Think further about who might be a stakeholder in this conversation. Is it medical doctors? Gender Studies professors? Environmentalists? Political scientists? For example, if teachers were doing research on and writing about your topic, then searching an "education" database might be helpful.

Once you begin to find relevant articles, you can often use those articles to find more articles. Look at the article's bibliography. Are any of those articles useful? Has the author written other articles? Has this journal published more articles on this topic? Who has cited the article you found? You can use tools (like Web of Science or Google Scholar) to see if an article has been cited or used as a source in other articles.

Popular, Special Interest, and Peer-Reviewed Sources

The Libraries' article databases include popular, special interest, and peer-reviewed articles or a mix. Many databases have capabilities to let you search by, or limit to, one type of source such as peer-reviewed journals. The table below can help you make sense of the range of source types and their characteristics.

	Popular	Special Interest	Scholarly or Peer-Reviewed
Lengths of articles	Short articles (1-2 pages)	Longer articles (5-10 pages)	Extensive articles (15-40 pages)
Who writes the articles?	Written by journalists. Uses straightforward language.	Written by practitioners or those in the field. Uses conversational and some specialized language.	Written by faculty members, scholars, or researchers. Uses complex language and jargon.
Where did the author get their information?	Focus is on timely reporting, few or no bibliography of sources	Often include a few research or scholarly sources in bibliography	Researchers collect new data and include a long bibliography (or footnotes), which places new discoveries in context.
How can you use them?	Facts, statistics, example opinions, trends	Statistics, trends, often include links to scholarly articles	New research discoveries and theories. These articles are considered the "gold standard" of academic publishing because they go through critical evaluation before being published.
Examples	New York Times, Newsweek, CNN, Sports Illustrated	Harvard Business Review, Dissent, Scientific American, Archaeology	Journal of Religion, Developmental Psychology, New England Journal of Medicine

Analyzing Sources

As you work with the sources you find, you can see how authors create or fit into debates within the conversation. Authors of articles always have a point and design their texts strategically to convince others. In many cases, useful sources offer you new ideas or information and use evidence that can help you develop or deepen your ideas about the topic. In the same way, reading an article is like listening to a conversation between the author and the sources they found and used to build their perspective. Your thoughts and judgments about texts you read are worthwhile, so your role as a researcher is to question them and ultimately join the conversation in an active way.

Analyzing a source is an active approach to reading. It includes critiquing the author's arguments and evidence, asking questions of the text and being able to respond, whether you agree or disagree. It helps you consider how to use others' words and ideas in your writing. Ask yourself:

- Does the article make sense to you and seem useful for your project?

- Does the information appear to be well-researched or is it supported by questionable evidence?

- Is the author's point of view presented in a way that makes it seem objective and impartial? In what ways is it made to foreground or obscure the author's personal investments in the conversation? In terms of ethos, what is the author's institutional affiliation, education, or experience?

- When and where was the source published? Does this matter?

Helpful Strategies for Reading a Scholarly Article

1. Look at the structure of the article. Many research articles follow a specific format:

    - Abstract - summary of the article

    - Introduction - why the author did the research and why it is important

    - Methodology - how the author did the research

    - Results - what the author found

    - Discussion - what the findings mean

- Conclusion - can take different forms including takeaways, next steps, future research, summing up the argument presented
- Bibliography/Works Cited/References - whose research the author read and used

2. Before reading the entire article, read the abstract and conclusion for main points to see whether they relate to your research question.

3. If you decide the article might be useful, read more carefully to begin developing a set of notes on its content in relation to your ideas. It's not unusual to re-read an article several times.

Using Websites in Your Research

As you look at specific web sources, it is important to critically evaluate them. Using the criteria below, you can assess a wide variety of web sources such as blogs, op-ed pages, foundations, government sites, news outlets, and others. As you work through these questions you will be able to determine the credibility and potential usefulness of the source.

Currency
- When was the information published? Is it current or out of date?
- Can you find a date for when it was written?

Relevance
- Is the information in the source relevant to your topic and what you want to write about?
- Who is the intended audience (e.g., parents, doctors, scientists, general public)?

Authority
- Who is the author or creator? Who is the publisher or sponsor? Is there a way to contact that person?
- What is the author's experience, qualifications, or investment in the topic?
- What is the URL? Is it a .com? .org? .edu? .gov? What does this tell you about the source?

Accuracy
- Are the information and evidence well-documented and reliable?
- Does the tone foreground or obscure biases and the author's agenda?

Purpose
- What is the purpose of the source?
- Is the point of view objective? Impartial?
- Are there political, ideological, cultural, religious, or personal biases?
- Is the author making claims? Expressing opinions? Sharing facts?

Getting the Full Text

The University Libraries has over 100,000 subscriptions to different journals, magazines, and newspapers. Although you might use one tool to "search" for an article, you actually might need to connect to another tool or database to view the "full text." That is where the "Find It" buttons comes in. Click "Find It" to search all the other subscriptions and connect to the full text.

However, keep in mind the University doesn't have online access to every article ever published. If you find something through a library tool, on Google or Google Scholar, or if an instructor recommends an article and the University doesn't have it, **don't pay money for it.** Instead, you can get it through **Interlibrary Loan**. Simply fill out the online form and the article will be sent to you in an email.

U of M Library Resources

Intro to Library Research

The University Libraries have designed some basic information to give you an introduction to the libraries and to doing academic and library research. Some instructors set up a time to visit the Library for a workshop during class time. Others might require you to complete the online tutorial. Others might expect you to do this outside of class time. Regardless, there are many ways to learn more.

Help from Librarians 24/7

Librarians are a great resource for any question because they want to help you find the sources and information you need. Librarians are experts about the collections and online journals we have access to. They don't report back to your instructors and there are no dumb questions when it comes to research. You can get help in person at any of the Libraries, by email, phone, or chat with a librarian from the website (lib.umn.edu) 24/7. This is a great way to get help because you can get help in the middle of your research if you have a question or get stuck.

Tools to Help with Bibliographies

The University Libraries have a variety of tools to help with organizing your bibliography. If you do use a bibliography tool, be sure to double-check the output because all of the tools can make mistakes. Compare the citations both in-text and in your bibliography. They should have a similar look.

NOTES

NOTES

NOTES

NOTES

NOTES

Part IV

Documentation Style Guides

All writers and researchers are expected to document the works that contribute to our own writing. There are different styles for this documentation, and the style is dependent—for the most part—on scholarly discipline. In the humanities and social sciences, MLA and APA are the most commonly used styles. In your FYW class, your instructor might use one or both of these. However, other styles might be especially relevant for your work, so it's a good idea to look into your discipline's chosen style.

In this section, you'll find out more about the entities that create these standards, as well as how to use them in your writing. Both sections include guidelines for how to create in-text and end-of-work bibliographic material, as well as sample pages. While MLA and APA are different, we use them for the same purpose: to document our source material and to assist our readers. In addition, citation practices can also help you keep track of your sources. Ask your instructor or librarian about citation managers offered by the U of M.

MLA Documentation Style

The Modern Language Association is a professional organization for language and literature scholars. The current edition of their documentation style guide, the eighth of its kind, is used by many writing and English instructors.

MLA In-Text Citation

MLA's in-text citations include the author's last name (or whichever element comes first in the Works Cited entry) and a page number. Where the last name appears depends on how you phrase the sentence: either before the page number or in the written language of the text. For example:

> A CNN poll revealed that the race was closer than previously thought (Kristoff 45).

According to McKaren, the state's most recent profile of inmates, the number of men imprisoned is over ten times more than women (16).

According to Joseph Rice, "The US has the highest incarceration rate of any developed nation" (2).

An in-text citation should clearly guide readers to the Works Cited page, where full bibliographic material is included. There are a few special cases, which are outlined below.

Authors with the same last name:
Her speech appeared to move members of the audience, as many were seen crying and hugging one another (V. Vieira 3).

More than one work by the same author:
The American Medical Association was developed in 1847, where the delegates agreed on the first official standards for a medical degree (Crusoe, "Our History" 14).

Anonymous author or organization as author:
Ten thousand users in Seattle alone were reported to have downloaded the smartphone application (*Latest trend* 4).

Source with paragraph numbers:
In her summary of the event, Malia Oldroyd writes about the heightened tension and anxiety that was present in the area that day (par. 4).

Source without page numbers:
He describes the activists as "nature activists and educators by trade" (Cortez).

Novel, play, or poem:
Rich's language is appropriate here: "Silence can be a plan / rigorously executed / the blueprint to a life / It is a presence / it has a history a form" (87; vol. 1, ch. 2).

Time-based media:
Frida's explanation that, "Our community has strong ties" was most evident to the newcomers ("*Divided*" 00:02:13-14).

Idea attributable to more than one source:

> Study of the disease has grown rapidly in the last several years, Gutierrez points out, as funding increased for all medical universities (Gutierrez 10; Farrell 56).

List of Works Cited

MLA 8 has a new general method for creating Works Cited lists that can be universally applied to any type of source. This method is important to understand as it provides the foundation for all MLA source citations.

The new method is based on nine core elements, which are listed below. To create a citation, you work through the elements one at a time. However, your citation may not contain every element. For example, the book you're citing might not have "other contributors" or a "version" so can skip those elements. Note that elements 3–9 are referred to as a "Container."

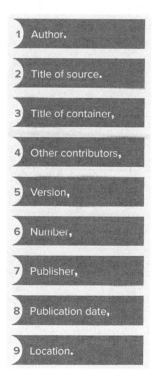

1. Author.

2. Title of source.

3. Title of container,

4. Other contributors,

5. Version,

6. Number,

7. Publisher,

8. Publication date,

9. Location.

Use the punctuation shown after each element.

Use the template on page 60 by inserting the information for each element of your source. Remember, your source might not have all elements.

You might need two containers if your source is retrieved through another source. For example, if you need to cite an NBC Television show that you streamed through Netflix, you have two containers: NBC and Netflix. If you need to cite an article from a journal that you accessed through a database, you have two containers: the journal and the database that contains the journal. See the example below, which shows how to handle two containers.

1 Author.	
2 Title of source.	"Canvassing."
CONTAINER 1	
3 Title of container,	*Parks and Recreation,*
4 Other contributors,	
5 Version,	
6 Number,	season 1, episode 2,
7 Publisher,	NBC,
8 Publication date,	16 April 2009.
9 Location.	
CONTAINER 2	
3 Title of container,	*Netflix,*
4 Other contributors,	
5 Version,	
6 Number,	
7 Publisher,	
8 Publication date,	
9 Location.	www.netflix.com/watch/20152006.

Fill out your template first, then look at the pages that follow for details on style and mechanics.

Remember, MLA creates citations by elements, not by individual types of sources. When you look at the following pages, be aware of the element you're in, not the type of source. For example, you will not find the subheading "painting" or "tweet" listed under each element. Instead, you will find different subheadings with examples that indicate where and how to properly abbreviate and punctuate.

1 Author.

One author:

> Squires, Laura. *Re-reading Feminist Zines*. University of Illinois P, 2002.

Two authors:

> Hamline, Judy, and Keith Fairband. "The Myth of the Man." *Gender and Profiles*, vol. 3, no. 1, Jan. 2012, pp. 14-38.

Three or more authors:

> Jenkins, John, et al. "Dealing with Bullies in College?" *Chicago Sun Times*, 13 Nov. 2015, p. 3.

Editor:

> Jokinen, Dale, editor. *Somewhere in the Name of God*. Amherst College P, 2011.

Two or more editors:

> Jokinen, Dale and Mary Kosira, editors. *Somewhere in the Name of God*. Amherst College P, 2011.
> Jokinen, Dale, et al., editors. *Somewhere in the Name of God*. Amherst College P, 2011.

Translator:

> Lazareva, Laura, translator. *Grips on the City: Trouble in Tangier*. By Simon Pardís, Drop Press, 2001.

Film and television:

Citations for film and television must begin with the individual's name whose contribution you are focusing on. For example, the author that created the first citation below was writing a paper about Tom Hardy's performance in the movie *Mad Max*.

> Hardy, Tom, performer. *Mad Max: Fury Road*. Village Roadshow, 2015.
> Miller, George, director. *Mad Max: Fury Road*. Village Roadshow, 2015.

Pseudonyms:

> @grammargirl. "KCSD rejects Common Core." Twitter, 12 July 2013, 3:41 p.m., twitter.com/grammargirl/2348230957.

Organization as author:

> National Public Radio. *NPR's This I Believe Essays*. Jezebel Press, 2013.

No author:

> "Rejecting the Common Core." Editorial. *St. Joseph News-Press,* 13 Jul. 2015, p. A2.

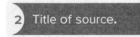

2 Title of source.

Book:

> Kosir, Mary. *Gearhead: Working with the Parts*. Duke UP, 2011.

Article in a periodical:

> Thenadi, Ramesh. "After the Spring." *Environmental Rhetoric,* vol. 12, no. 2, 2014, pp. 121-25.

Entire website:

> Winchell, Sarah. *The Social Scientista,* 2007-2016, thesocialscientista.com.

Posting on a website:

> Emerson, Ariana. "What Handwriting Does to the Brain."*ScientificAmerican*, 13 Nov. 2013, scientificamerican. com/2013>handwritingandthebrain/.

Entire Episode (TV):

> "The One with the Lost Shoes." *Friends*. Created by James Keegan, performance by Jennifer Aniston, season 6, episode 1, ABC, 2009.

Email:

> Use the subject line as a title.

> Lewis, Cecil. "Tasks for class." Received by Jan Jameson, 14 June 2016.

Untitled:

> Provide a generic description, capitalizing the first word and any proper nouns.

Collection:

> Mankameyer, Tera. "Righting the Water Wrongs." *Developing Digital Literacies*, edited by Susan Harding, U of Chicago P, 2015, pp. 134-69.

Periodical:

> Maresse, Dominic. "Fourth Wave Feminism?" *San Francisco Daily Register,* 13 Jul. 2016, p. 2A.

Entire Television series:

> "The One with the Lost Shoes." *Friends*. Created by James Keegan, performance by Jennifer Aniston, season 6, episode 1, ABC, 2009.

Translator:

> Kuhn, Jordan. *Dreaming of a Memory.* Translated by Samantha Erast, Freeglove Design Press, 2009.

Editor:

> Deleuze, Jueri. *Dissention of the West.* Edited by Hayden McCall, Brown Books, 2011.

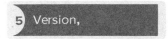
5 Version,

The Bible. Authorized King James Version, Oxford UP, 1998.

Wei, Bryan, and Jenny B. Helms. *Anti-American Counterpublics*, 2nd ed., Times Press, 2012.

Granger, Tyrion. *Helm's Deep*. 1999. Performance by Barbara Whitaker, director's cut, Warner Bros., 2001.

6 Number,

Poage, Alice. *Redrawing the Line: Redistricting Rights*. 2nd ed., vol. 2, York UP, 2004.

Cunningham, Laura. "Defeating the Odds: Ethnographic Study of Homeless Youth." *EthnoMethods*, vol.1, no. 1, Jan 2015, pp. 23-49.

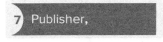
7 Publisher,

Book:
Frank, Edie. *Militant Counterpublics*. Northwestern UP, 2012.

Films and television series:
Pizzolatto, Nic, creator. *True Detective*. Anonymous Content, 2014.

Websites:
Stop the Fight: Campaign Against Bullying, National Institute for Public Health, Washington, DC, stopthefight.org/index/caskj34.

8 Publication date,

Article on a news website:
Marchesa, Tia. "Dealing with the Right from the Left." *USA Today*, 23 June 2015, www.usatoday/magazine/archive/2015/dealing-with-the-right/24908/.

Print article:

> Marchesa, Tia. "Dealing with the Right from the Left." *USA Today*,
> May-June 2015, pp. 13-19.

Issue of a periodical:

> Gramsci, Henry. "Steinbeck and the Difficult Art." *Lit Discussion*,
> vol. 110, no. 2, Spring 2009, pp. 35-47.

9 Location.

Page numbers:

> Meza, Maria. "Reading Vines Rhetorically." *PreText*, vol. 120, no. 2,
> Apr. 2015, pp. 122-145.

URL:

> Travant, Louis. "The Baby Boomers Have Left the Building." *How
> Life Works*, 15 Feb. 2016, www.howlifeworks.com/pod2934/
> htm.

DOI:

> Chen, Andrew. "In One's Own Hand: Seeing Manuscripts in a
> Digital Age." *Digital Humanities Quarterly*, vol. 6, no. 3, July
> 2014. Project Muse, doi:10.1016/j.ssresearch.2011.04.012.

Place:

> Warhol, Andy. *Campbell's Soup Cans*. 1962, Museum of Modern
> Art, New York.

Venue and city:

> Noble, Morgan. "The Planets of Identity." TED Conference, 18 Nov.
> 2013, Reisner Hotel, Chicago.

MLA Practice Template

1. Author.
2. Title of source.

CONTAINER 1

3. Title of container,
4. Other contributors,
5. Version,
6. Number,
7. Publisher,
8. Publication date,
9. Location.

CONTAINER 2

3. Title of container,
4. Other contributors,
5. Version,
6. Number,
7. Publisher,
8. Publication date,
9. Location.

From *MLA Handbook* (8th ed.), published by the Modern Language Association (style.mla.org).

APA Documentation Style

The American Psychological Association is a scientific and professional organization for psychologists. Their documentation style, despite the name, is often used by scholars in social and behavioral sciences. Currently in its sixth edition of the manual, these materials reflect the information.

APA In-Text Citation

APA's in-text citations include the author's last name, the date of publication, and the location of the source material. Where this information appears depends on how you want to phrase the sentences. The in-text citation should guide readers to the References page, where full bibliographic material is included. More on this in the next section.

Basic format for a quotation:
> Buchanan (2005) demonstrated that the AIDS crisis "lasted longer than most Americans remember" (p. 4).

Basic format for a summary or a paraphrase:
> O'Hara and Brandt's (2009) work with children in rural South Dakota indicates that there are a number of factors, aside from language, that influence reading ability in school settings.

Work with two authors:
> Hauser and Strauss (2011) contend that, "In language acquisition, the optimal learning window has been a matter of huge contention amongst scholars" (p. 23).

Work with three to five authors:
> In 2014, Klein, Morgan, and Kronkite suggested that the new curriculum model be used for early childhood learning outcomes (p. 65).

Work with six or more authors:
> Klein et al. (2003) addressed the argument that researchers construct a "gap" in the literature, creating a metaphor of physical space in which to submit their work (p. 75).

Work with unknown author:
> In San Francisco, young people ages 18-24 are the fastest growing homeless population ("Millennials," 2015).

Organization as author:

> Studies show that podcasts can help kids and adults improve their reading skills (National Public Radio [NPR], 2014).

Authors with the same last name:

> J. Jones (2000) argues…
> K. Jones (2004) disagrees…

Two or more works by the same author in the same year:

> Hahn (2012b) advances a binary from which to approach classical rhetoric, one concerned with rewriting history and another with appropriating it.

Two or more works in the same parentheses:

> The groups are characterized as subordinate to a dominant public organized by the circulation of discourse (Fraser, 1992; Warner, 2002; Asen & Brouwer, 2001).

Multiple citations to the same work in one paragraph:

> As soon as we began, Anne Rooney compared her new fitness regimen to what she had done previously. "It's completely different. It's more structured and you feel more of a community-base, which keeps you on track" (personal communication, May 3, 2015). When I asked Rooney to tell me a little bit about the community she explained that the volunteer opportunities often connect gym members with the local community (Rooney, 2015).

Web source:

> Tremblay (1999) explains how ideology can be placed at the center of the classroom to allow students to externalize false consciousness.

> No page numbers:
> The President was joined by members of Congress, many of whom were said to be "far less than pleased" about the morning's events (Barnes, 2016, para 4).

Unknown author:
A person's BMI can be used to screen for health problems that may occur as a result of excess weight ("BMI," 2014).

Unknown date:
The Declaration of Human Rights was the first expression of rights for all citizens around the world (Quaid, n.d.).

An entire website:

The U.S. Department of Housing and Urban Development website (http://portal.hud.gov/hudportal/HUD) provides a wealth of resources for disaster preparation.

Multivolume work:

Wayne (1986) points out the ethnographic study of protected populations is no longer a possibility for researchers (Volume 2, p. 131).

Personal communication:

The process of the interview was much more taxing than expected for Shonda, so we scheduled more time in between our meetings (S. Rhimes, personal communication, June 24, 2014).

Course materials:

Cite as personal communication.

Part of a source:

The findings do not support the decision to prosecute the defendant as an adult (Jacobson, Table 4.2, p. 68).

Indirect source:

Quinn Harris' qualms with community are similar: "It often presents the language and conventions of writing as unproblematic and cohesive…" (as cited in Sanders, 2013, p. 34).

Sacred or classical text:

On his side he has a tattoo that cites his favorite Bible verse: "May I never boast except in the Cross of our Lord Jesus Christ" (Galatians 6:14, Standard Version).

List of References

In APA, your "References" belong on a separate page at the end of your work. General guidelines for the References page as follows. First find the type of source you're working with, then create the citation according to the example offered.

Single author:
> Wright, T. (2012). *Literacy and social change*. Pittsburgh, PA: University of Pittsburgh Press.

Two to seven authors:
> Elmberg, K., Anderson, Q., & Yates, B. (2009). Writing and controversy. *College Composition and Communication, 41*, 1365-1387.

Eight or more authors:
> Chu, D., Sanders, M., Teston, T., Hanten, J., Graham, L., Krych, R.,...Felice, A. (2013). Written dissent a community of strangers. *College Composition, 42*, 432-500.

Organization as author:
> American Psychiatric Association. (2014). *Handbook of mental disorders* (4th ed.). New York, NY: Author.

Unknown author:
> *The world of paper*. (2015). Chicago, IL: Fallwell Press.

Author using a pseudonym or screen name:
> Orginos. (2015, December 2). Systems of socialization [Comment]. *The Atlantic*. Retrieved from http://www.theatlantic.ghytx.com/

Two or more works by the same author:
> Cruz, C. (2001). *American indiscretion*. Cambridge, England: Cambridge University Press.
> Cruz, C. (2015). *The rise of the righteous queens*. Cambridge, England: Cambridge University Press.

Two or more works by the same author in the same year:

> Crane, B. (2014a, March). New takes on clinic treatment. *Anthropology Quarterly, 143(1),* 4-18.
> Crane, B. (2014b, September). Revisiting the new takes. *Anthropology Quarterly, 143*(3), 3-16.

Editor:

> Bethers, D. & Sheard, V. (Eds.). (2001). *The trouble with causing trouble.* Portsmouth, NH: Boynton/Cook Publishers, Inc.

Author and editor:

> Grable, H. (2012). *Qualitative research in Rwanda.* Feliz, R. (Ed.). Seaside, CA: Trig Publications. (Original work published in 1999)

Translator:

> Trede, K. (2004). *Hebrew beginnings.* (F. Gibbons, Trans.). Oxford, UK: Oxford University Press. (Original work published 1990)

Editor and translator:

> Tomazewski, P. & Larpenteur, L. (Ed.). (2006). *The sophistic politic.* (G. L. Warren, Trans.) Urbana, IL: University of Illinois Press. (Original work published 1983)

Article in a journal:

> Chen, A. (2012). In one's own hand: Seeing manuscripts in a digital age. *Digital Humanities Quarterly, 6*(2), 59-73. doi:10.1016/j.ssresearch.2011.04.012

Article in a magazine:

> Delaney, T. (2015, January 4). What's the deal with term limits? *Political American, 43*(3), 28-34.

Article in a newspaper:

> Humphreys, C. M. (2013, October 4). The best kind of homeless. *Chicago Sun Times.* Retrieved from http://chicagosuntimes.ref4560.com

Abstract:

Del Toro, G. & Triavé, J. (2009). Working functions in the frontal lobe of Alzheimer's patients [Abstract]. *Journal of Modern Medicine, 110*, 220-221. Retrieved from http://sciencedirect.com

Supplemental material:

Tubbs, G. & Russell, F. (2013). The socialism in social movement scholarship [Supplemental material]. *Rhetorica, 112*(3). doi:10.1016/j.ssresearch.20113.04.01

Article with a title in its title:

Kitteridge, O. (2007). The effects of women's "role in the home" on 20th century economic policy. *Economic Endeavors,* 14-21. doi:10.239/eced12247

Letter to the editor:

Eggers, R. (2015, October). [Letter to the editor]. *Medium.* Retrieved from http://www.medium.ghr3q.leted.com

Editorial or other unsigned article:

Dealing with bullies in college? [Editorial]. (2016, January 15). *The New York Times.* Retrieved from http://www.thenewyorktimes.com

Newsletter article:

Oberlin, E. (n.d.). Why Americans love juicing. *Dietary Review, 12.* Retrieved from http://www.dietaryreview.juicing.54ag/asp=127

Review:

Adams, V. (2015). [Review of the book *Living with AIDS,* by H. Jameson]. *Health and Disease 43,* 19-22. doi:10.2342/gysd/23872

Published interview:

Winfrey, O. (2011, May 20). A conversation with Oprah Winfrey [Interview by Manuel]. *Vogue.* Retrieved from http://www.vogue.com

Article in a reference work (encyclopedia, dictionary, wiki):

Autoethnography. (2007). In *Blackwell encyclopedia of sociology* (Vol. 1, pp. 260-263). Newark, NJ: Range Publications.

Comment on an online article:

riotgrrrl90. (2000). The mess of the patriarchy [Comment]. *Bustle*. Retrieved from http://www.bustle.com/fr32ay

Testimony before a legislative body:

Riggs, Howard. (2012, Jan 5). *Addressing disability concerns for online forums*. Testimony before the Subcommittee on Postsecondary Writing Instruction. Retrieved from http://www.pswi.edu/ha4256.html

Paper presented at a meeting or symposium (unpublished):

Tivol, J. E. (2013, May 17). *Listening on the margins*. Paper presented at the Conference on Bordered Health Concerns, Tempe, AZ.

Poster session at a conference:

Gross, H. (2015, March 10). *What's social about media?* Poster session presented at the Conference on Millennial Perspectives, Charlotte, NC.

Basic format for a book:

Print:

Herrod, S. (2001). *Brains for sale*. New York, NY: Cortez Publishers.

Web:

Sikhan, J. (2014). The Rwandan genocide. Retrieved from http://books.google.com

E-book:

Logan, C. (2016). Dealing with determinism. [Kindle version]. Retrieved from http://amazon.com

Database:
Chavra, D. (2014). Injustice on the equator: The coffee games. Retrieved from http://muse.umn.edu/

Edition other than the first:

Bajarwaj, R. (2013). *The new yogic tradition* (2nd ed.) Irvine, CA: Travail Press.

Selection in an anthology or collection

Entire anthology:
Krasinski, E. (Ed.). (2014). *The rhetorics of collection.* Boulder, CO: University of Colorado Press.

Selection in an anthology:
Franks, S. (2014). The rhetoric of NASCAR. In E. Krasinski (Ed.). *The rhetorics of collection* (pp. 34-56). Boulder, CO: University of Colorado Press.

Multivolume work:

All volumes:
Guiducci, L. (2010). *Metacognitive awareness in elementary education* (Vols. 1-3). Chicago, IL: DePaul University.

One volume, with title:
Sims, D. (2007). *Geometrical solutions to urban development: Vol. 1.* Minneapolis: University of Minnesota Press.

Introduction, preface, foreword, or afterword

Lykins, M. (2015). Foreword. In G. T. Quail, *Getting gone* (pp. v-vii). Boston, MA: Grave Press.

Dictionary or other reference work:

All volumes:
Swarts, C. (2000). *Encyclopedia of childhood learning* (Vols. 1-4). Stamford, CT: Vortex.

One volume, with title
Stein, V. (2004). *A brief dictionary of rhetoric.* Ithaca, NY: Hairston Press.

Republished book:

> Tognazzini, O. (2010). *The analytics of coding language.*
> Greenwich, CT: Webbed. (Original work published
> 1989)

Book with a title in its title:

> Hart-Davis, E. (2013). *Expressions of* A Thousand Plateaus
> *in a French community.* Thousand Oaks, CA: Sage.

Book in a language other than English:

> Trédé, M. (1992). *Kairos.* [Kairos]. Paris, France: Klincsieck.

Dissertation:

> Published:
>
> Weaver, P. (2015). *Intercultural dimensions in one local
> community* (Doctoral dissertation). Available from
> ProQuest Dissertations and Theses database. (AAT
> 239806)
>
> Unpublished:
>
> Hooker, C. (2008). *Othering the border: Whitewashing in
> south Texas* (Unpublished doctoral dissertation).
> University of South Texas, Houston, TX.

Conference proceedings:

> Mottola, T. (2014). Challenging the divide in Rwanda.
> In *Proceedings of African Institute Conference.*
> Retrieved from http://aic.net:23409/program/
> proceedings/

Government document:

> U.S. Food and Drug Administration. (2014). *Depression
> and suicide in patients being treated
> with antidepressants: FDA public health
> advisory.* Retrieved from http://www.fda.gov/
> medicineresearch-press/2014/

Report from a private organization:

> Human Rights Watch. (2013, November). *Initiative for
> budget tracking in rural areas of developing
> countries.* Retrieved from http://www.
> humanrightswatch.org/pdfs/lib/budget/

Legal source:

> Plessy v. Ferguson, 163 U.S. 537 (1896). Retrieved from Cornell University Law School, Legal Information Institute website: http://www.law.cornell.edu/supremecourt/text/163/53

Sacred or classical text:

> Sacred texts such as the Bible or Qur'an and classical Greek or Roman texts are not cited in the list of references.

Entire website:

> Entire websites should not be cited in the list of references. Give the URL in parentheses when it's mentioned in the text of your paper.

Document from a website:

> Matsukane, D. & Froage, K. (2013, January). Ethnographic measures in the Middle East. Retrieved from Cornell University website: http://cornell.edu/research/gwto33/measures

Section in a web document:

> Sutherland, U. (2013, July). Facial recognition software for air travel. In *Security for the future*. Retrieved from National Institute of Technology website: http://nit.org/catalog/sjde23445

Blog post:

> Ramirez, J. (2016, May 5). It's never what you think it should be with these guys [Blog post]. Retrieved from http://www.therightwatch.com/its-never-what-you-think/klwelt33

Blog comment:

> trivialnational. (2016, May 18). What about hashtag sustainability, bro? [Blog comment]. Retrieved from http://www.chronicle.com/blogs/the-paper-part/hastag.sustainability.bro/

Podcast:

> Koenig, S. (2015). *Serial* [Audio podcast]. Retrieved from http://serialpodcast.org

Video or audio on the web:

> Huber, J. (2013). *Cooking with kids*. [Video file]. Retrieved from http://www.youtube.com/watch?v239482

Transcript of an audio or video file:

> Perreault, G. F. (2015). *How the USPS got started* [Transcript of video file]. Retrieved from http://www.materialhistory.org/usps-start2349

Film:

> Crowley, J. (Director). (2015). *Brooklyn* [Motion picture]. Los Angeles, CA: Fox Searchlight Pictures.

Television or radio program:

> Series:
>
> Glazer, I. (Executive Producer). (2014). Broad City [Television series]. New York, NY: Comedy Central.
>
> Episode:
>
> Imperioli, M. (Writer), & Buscemi, S. (Director). (2002). Everybody hurts [Television series episode]. In D. Chase (Executive Producer), *The Sopranos*. New York, NY: Home Box Office.

Music recording:

> Knowles, Beyoncé. (2016). *Lemonade* [CD]. New York, NY: Columbia Records.

Lecture, speech, or address:

> Wallace, D. F. (2005, May 21). *This is water*. Address at Kenyon Commencement. Gambier, OH.

Data set or graphic representation of data:

> Gallup (2015, November). *Republican reactions to the governor's race over time* [Data set]. Retrieved from http://gallup.com/2349/governors-race-over-time

Mobile app or software:

> Headspace. [Mobile application software]. (2016). Retrieved from http://itunes.apple.com/

Video game:
> Relativity Media. (2000). Fortress [Video game]. San Diego, CA: Graham. PlayStation.

Map:
> Reservations of the pacific northwest. [Map]. (2009). Retrieved from http://nairms.org/nativeamerican-reservation-maps/23049j

Advertisement:
> Nike [Advertisement]. (2015, September). *Marie Claire, 70*(3), 13.

Work of art or photograph:
> Dali, S. (1931). *The persistence of memory* [Painting]. Museum of Modern Art, New York, NY.

Brochure or fact sheet:
> National Medical Council. (1999). *Signs of a heart attack* [Fact sheet]. Retrieved from http://nationalmedicalcouncil.com/archives/pdf23496

Press release:
> Peace Women. (2016, March). *The gentrification of women's rights* [Press release]. Retrieved from http://peacewomen.org/pub/bitly/23499.htm

Presentation slides:
> Eischens, V. A. (2014). *Writing with DITA* [Presentation slides]. Retrieved from http://codex.com/catalog/g239bit

Lecture notes or other course materials:
> Hoemke, L. (2015). Case studies of professional writers [Lecture notes and audio file]. In L Hoemke & S. Rabban, *The written profession.* Retrieved from http://usc.eml.edu/gls212

Email:
> Emails, letters, and other personal communications are not cited in the list of references.

Archived online posting:

> Garman, A. (2009, October 10). Gaming the system [Electronic mailing list message]. Retrieved from http://www.trap.mailchimp/system/2009/23948.html

Twitter post (tweet):

> Bourdain [Anthony]. (2014, June 16). This airport burger did not cause me to fall into a spiral of depression. [Tweet]. Retrieved from http://twitter.com/alkwerobourdaina/234235

Facebook post:

> U.S. Department of Agriculture. (2015, September 2). Young Farmers Harvest Coalition [Facebook post]. Retrieved May 14, 2016, from http://www.facebook.com/AG.gov

Part V

Student Writing

This section presents several recent winners of the Excellence in First-Year Writing Award and the Scott Jacobson Spirit Award. These examples of excellence are chosen to suggest the range and diversity of writing that students create in FYW classes and to showcase multiple forms that excellence can take in writing. When many people first hear about a writing award in an academic setting, they might picture the "perfect paper" that fulfills all of the conventions of writing that past experience taught them to think of as correct. In contrast, as students learn in First-Year Writing classes, real writing is not a matter of blindly attempting to reproduce a mythical perfect paper or force words and ideas into a one-size-fits-all framework. Instead, writing is a matter of actively making decisions about how to develop and explain ideas. Just as the range of human experiences and ideas exhibit wide-ranging variety, the expression, exploration, and explanations will properly represent differences as well. As you read these essays, then, seek not to hear one voice speaking in one way. Instead, we invite you to seek real writing—different people communicating in different ways about their own, and our collective, experiences and understandings of the world we share.

▮ College Pro Painters for Life
By Brady Becker

In "College Pro Painters for Life," Brady Becker tells the story of a summer job and the lessons it taught him. As you read the essay, ask yourself how Becker brings the story to life for readers and helps us relate to his experience. As you think about this, notice the way the essay balances dialogue with description and uses details such as character's names, actual products, and quotes from characters that represent their personalities.

College Pro Painters for Life

It was hot. The type of hot that makes you want to take a bath in the Antarctic Ocean or eat a box of popsicles all in succession. The type of hot that leaves a sharp red burn on your neck that bites for days. Sweat stained our faces, trickled down our backs, and seeped through all areas of our clothing. Countless drips and streaks of a deep purple stain decorated our bodies. Even our once white bandanas had become a canvas for our summer's work, speckled with drops of paint from an array of different jobs we had completed. Three inch paint brush held firmly in one hand, 5 gallon paint bucket in the offer, shirts tossed aside, flip flops barely covering our feet, and dirty rags tucked in our athletic shorts: Garritt and I were doing what we did all of that summer of 2012 - paint.

"This watermelon is my best friend... not even kidding right now dude," Garritt said to me as he passionately took another bite from the juicy melon.

"Bro... I kind of thought we were best friends though?" I replied as I wiped the excess succulent juices from underneath my chin.

"You dude? No man, were just co-workers. You're just somebody to talk to while I get my paint stroke on, know what I'm sayin'?"

"I see how it is then," I laughed, "you only like me for my watermelon."

"Exactly!" Garritt came back. Our often extended lunch breaks were typically the highlight of the day. It gave us a chance to escape the suffocating heat, unwind, and just talk.

"How much of that underside of the deck do you think we have left?" I asked changing subjects.

"Ahhh I don't know man, at least another 6 hours of work for the each of us. We are already over budget hours too..."

"Really, that much left? Dangit, we're over budget hours again dude?"

"Yeah man, same old song and dance. Underpaid and overworked," Garritt laughed.

"I think you're wrong dude! This deck will only take us another 3 hours or so as long as we cut down on our five minute breaks," I said sarcastically.

Garritt was wrong. The underside of the deck took us another 10 hours of work each. We finished the job almost 20 hours over budget. Our base salary was minimum wage, so if we exceeded the given amount of budget hours for a project, we earned below minimum wage. In other words, Garritt and I had slaved over this project in the soaking sun for three full days of work for not even six dollars an hour pay. The system was flawed. The budget hours assigned were notoriously under-estimated. Garritt and I always used to joke that not even Sherwin Williams himself could beat the budget. At the end of that project, much like many others, we went home with nothing but skimpy paychecks and heads full of deep purple stained hair.

Just 6 months prior, this painting gig had seemed so attractive and adventurous. Garritt and I were interviewed at a dingy McDonald's across town. At the time, nothing seemed peculiar about a professional job interview being held at a fast food joint, but an apprehensive thought never crossed our minds. While deep fryers sizzled in the background, Nic Rintoul, our soon to be boss, swindled us into believing the endless opportunity and wonderful employment that his company, College Pro Painters, had to offer.

"College Pro Painters – together, realizing potentials. The logo is blue boys because that's the same color as the sky and with College Pro Painters – the sky's the limit. You'll start making 10 dollars an hour with a chance to make even more, you decide when you want to work, and you'll be working outside with your friends. What more could you want?" Nic always used to preach this to us. Even though we soon found out that Nic Rintoul was a crooked businessman, we had to give the man one concession. He was one hell of a salesman. Nic could sell a pork dinner to an orthodox Jew. And at the same place where happy meals were being sold, Nic sold us. At that very moment Garritt and I shared the excitement of the preschoolers frolicking in the sticky ball pit as we proudly shook Nic Rintoul's hand and officially became College Pro Painters.

What ensued over the course of our 9 month employment with College Pro Painters was completely unpredictable. Garritt and I performed numerous assignments that were never described by our boss in the job description. We went door to door, marketing for College Pro Painters, pointing out far-fetched paint defects at people's houses, and made empty guarantees such as "Yes, we are bona fide, highly trained, professional painters" or "Yeah, contrary to popular belief you can actually paint over vinyl". We hadn't the slightest clue how to market something we had never in fact performed ourselves. However, after weeks and weeks of feeble doormat sale pitches, Garritt and I began to come into our own as paint job peddlers. Behind our confident smiles and sweet words, we truly had minimal knowledge of the painting industry, but we were convincing. People bought into our phony poise and purchased our painting services along with it.

Marketing for College Pro Painters was a challenge but the actual task of painting was the real struggle. Customers expected a professionally done job as we had personally guaranteed. Much to customer's dissatisfaction, expectations were often left unfulfilled that summer. Having being trained by Nic Rintoul in an 8 hour crash course in College Pro Painter fundamentals, Garritt and I's painting skills remained rather rudimentary. Nic instilled catch phrases into us such as "be systematic", "fast and efficient, beat budget", and "okey dokes, good enough" and although Garritt and I found great amusement out of mimicking Nic's ludicrous one-liners all summer long, his amateur teaching set us up for inevitable failures.

With lack of proper training, Garritt and I honed our painting skills through a series of trials and tribulations. At first, Garritt and I tried to truly embrace the Nic Rintoul slogan of "fast and efficient work". However, our aimless efforts mutated fast and efficient into mediocre and clumsy. Paint drops from our brushes often permanently scarred customer's concrete driveways, their streak less windows, and unscathed vinyl siding. Coupled with our naive craftsmanship was our blatant inability to paint any sort of exterior trim. Whether it was a clear-cut window trim or the edge of a soffit Garritt and I painted much like kindergartens color, outside the lines. All of these woeful slip-ups left our customers disappointed to say the very least.

Yet, oddly enough, somewhere in between the crummy paychecks and lackadaisical painting errors in the dead heat of summer, Garritt and I grew a keen love for the College Pro Painters lifestyle. Our repetitive failures fueled a whole new spirited motivation. Painting became more than just a paycheck, it was a passion. Suddenly, the money had lost its meaning. Despite suffering docks in pay, Garritt and I genuinely wanted to do a professional level job for our customers. Practice hadn't made perfect, but our painting skills had become respectable. And although our best efforts still weren't exemplary, customers took notice of our admirable work ethic and steadfast passion.

"Mr. and Mrs. Kovorski, we would like once again just to sincerely apologize for the spots of paint that have tarnished your vinyl siding beneath the deck. We did our best to remove the stains, but unfortunately there's nothing more we can really do. We are real pleased with how the deck turned out and we will talk to our boss about a partial refund in regards..." Garritt started before the homeowner interrupted. Apologies had become a part of the job that summer.

"Fellas, don't worry about the little oopsies underneath the deck. We know you boys work too long and hard for little scrap to fuss over a few drips of paint. You fellas really did a bang-up job and you've got a coupla bright futures ahead of you," Mr. Kovorski interjected as he handed us each a fat $40 dollar tip.

Garritt and I were both so taken aback that we were barely to able manage exchanges of gratitude. We weren't used to this sort of money. More rewarding than the monetary incentive, however, was the radiant smile in which Mrs. Kovorski was advertising. Her smile conveyed satisfaction, and even a hint of appreciation. We felt the warmth and acceptance of a community behind it. A simple smile had never felt so good to Garritt and me.

The official College Pro Painters website cites the company's central mission is "to embrace challenge, innovate, and excel" (College Pro Painters). Regardless of all Nic's empty promises, our deliberate customer deception, long hours with little pay, and countless painting blunders, Garritt and I's summer as College Pro Painters blossomed into a tremendous learning experience. Garritt and I embraced the challenge of learning foreign concepts such as marketing door to door, customer service, managing a small scale operation, and all things painting. We innovated by developing personable relationships with customers and passionately painting above the College Pro questionable standards. Through the process of this all, Garritt and I excelled. We developed stern work ethics, emerged as effective leaders, grasped the importance of responsibility, established working relationships with customers and had become even closer friends. We had excelled as business men, friends, and as individuals overall. As College Pro Painters, together, Garritt and I were able to realize our infinite potentials.

■ Advertising Appeals and the Perfect Pair of Jeans
By Daniel Picardo

In his essay "Advertising Appeals and the Perfect Pair of Jeans," Daniel Picardo interprets and analyzes a magazine advertisement for men's jeans. As you read the essay, think about how Picardo invites his readers to connect with his topic through the opening paragraphs. In addition, notice how the essay develops its thesis in stages, beginning with the relatively simple "it's not what you have that's important . . .it's what people think of what you have," to the more developed statement that ends the second paragraph beginning with the phrase "But this paper will show." In the body of the essay, notice how Brown combines different kinds of writing including description, interpretation, analysis, and incorporation of outside sources.

Advertising Appeals and the Perfect Pair of Jeans

I was in the fourth grade when I realized that your clothes are not just your clothes. I was nine, and starting a new year, at a new school, in a new state. I had no friends and no idea what to expect, but one of the first things I learned was that if I wanted to be liked, I had to wear FILA. I had no idea what FILA was; I didn't know whether it was an abbreviation, an acronym, a sports team, or something else entirely. I had no frame of reference for the brand except that I knew the most popular students in my class all wore shoes, jackets, and hats emblazoned with FILA's distinctive logo and color scheme. And I knew that I wanted some. I know now that it's a clothing company named after two Italian brothers (History of Fila), and that the reason I wanted them was not because of the clothes themselves, but because other people had them and I wanted to be a part of their group. I didn't learn those things that year, though. Instead I learned other things, like long division, that the peregrine falcon is the fastest creature on earth, and that it isn't what you have that's important… it's what people think of what you have.

Reading that paragraph, perhaps you laughed at your own similarities of discovery, or reminisced about that one item you just *had* to have in your grade school days, and you may have, for a moment, thought, "I'm glad those days are behind me." But this paper will show, through a close examination of an advertisement for the Lee Jeans Company, that the desire to attain a social class is still very much a part of everyday adult life, and that while the techniques of inspiring that desire have become more subtle, they have also become more complex, moving from simple appeals for clothing brands to appeals based on gender roles and socio-economic status.

The advertisement we will be examining is a half-page magazine ad featuring an attractive man wearing mainstream casual clothing, holding a coffee cup and leaning against a yellow car, while an equally attractive woman, with whom he is making eye contact, walks by in the background (Lee 25). At the top of the page, in an orange header with white lettering, is the phrase, "Comfort Never Looked So Good" and "The New Lee Modern Series," accompanied by the Lee logo. At first glance, however, we cannot tell what product this ad is selling. This tells us that the jeans themselves are clearly not the primary selling point of this ad, but rather that the advertiser must be intending the imagery to convey some other message about the jeans – what one marketing strategist describes as an emotional appeal, where the "graphic elements of the message itself speak to consumers through a subconscious language" (Orwig). But what is the presented message?

Looking for meaning in these subconscious signifiers, the first thing that stands out is the bold yellow car the man is leaning against. You see only a portion of the vehicle, but it is enough to suggest the aggressive lines and oversized engineering of an American sports car. This stands in juxtaposition to the cup of coffee the man holds, which is small and virtually non-descript, a white cup in a brown cardboard sleeve – though the cup itself could stand as a subtle indicator that the man buys coffee from a shop, having the money to pay a premium for something simple. Together these images speak of a man who is interested in the finer things of life, but with a firm moderation; this a man who does not grasp for more than he needs, but knows what he wants. Furthermore, he is positioned before an urban storefront, indicating that he is also sophisticated and worldly, at home and comfortable in a big city; these aren't farmers' or cowboys' jeans. While any one of these images could individually be taken as incidental, when taken as a whole, they provide a very clear image of the social status Lee wants consumers to associate with its jeans. This becomes even more significant when viewed in light of a report published by the American Marketing Association that determined "[s]ocial status is one dimension...that is likely to influence consumers' feelings of distinctiveness and their advertising response," and that "social status involves consumers' perceptions of the relative position of groups in society based on a particular characteristic" (Grier and Deshpandé 217). Or in this case, a set of characteristics which defines both the man and the ad's target consumer, and shapes the perceived value of each in relation to other groups.

The final prominent element to analyze in this ad is the role of the woman in subconscious communication. She is well-dressed, and well-styled, with clothing and jewelry that look expensive. Her face and posture are both open, calm, and relaxed. The movement of her hair gives the indication that she is in motion, walking by the man, and her face is turned toward him, showing that she is taking note of him as she passes. She is self-assured, attractive, confidently on her way to somewhere, and the man not only catches her attention, but returns her interest, and they share a flirtation in the brief moment captured in this ad. Some might argue that since she isn't overtly sexualized, her role could be to appeal indirectly to the women who will see this ad, to give them a point of association which might be intriguing enough to buy the jeans for a man in her life, which is the argument made in a 1995 study which found that when women were shown advertising images of romance and courtship they "became emotionally involved in these ads, able to self-project to a tremendous degree and to create imaginative stories about the people portrayed in the [them]" (Williams). While that could be a valid interpretation in many such ads, I would disagree with that intention in this one. I disagree for the simple reason that this woman has no interaction with the advertised product whatsoever; her vantage does not offer her any view of the man's pants, and she is in fact separated from the man by one of his own possessions. The incongruity of those observations is only further exaggerated by another: that the jeans themselves are never completely represented in the ad. They are shown, but there are no details to make them stand out, you cannot see the full silhouette or waistline, and there is not even one unobstructed view of one leg. Assuming it were actually possible for her to see them, there is nothing about the jeans for the woman to notice! Considering those facts, it is clear that the woman, rather than being an individual character or a romantic interest, has become just another aspect of affirmation for the consumer, a set piece to further indicate the social status of the man and, by extension, the jeans and the consumer himself.

On its face, this ad is selling modern, comfortable, and good looking jeans by the Lee Jeans Company. My argument is that this ad isn't selling jeans at all. It is selling a lifestyle. The product is almost incidental, in fact, to achieving the societal standing you desire, rather like a ticket for a train. When you buy the ticket, it isn't the paper you want, but the destination. In the same way this ad isn't about jeans, it's about social status and perceptions of sophistication, attraction, and popularity. Or perhaps more succinctly: it's about what people think of what you have.

Works Cited

Grier, Sonya A. and Deshpandé, Rohit. "Social Dimensions of Consumer Distinctiveness: The Influence of Social Status on Group Identity and Advertising Persuasion." *Journal of Marketing Research* 38.2 (2001): 216-224. Web. 3 Mar. 2015.

"History of Fila." *FILA*. n.p., 2014. Web. 3 Mar. 2015.

Lee. Advertisement. Popular Science Oct. 2014: 25. Print.

Orwig, Ken. "Rational Appeals vs. Emotional Appeals in Advertising and Marketing Communication." *Orwig Marketing Strategies*. n.d. Web. 3 Mar. 2015.

Williams, Patti. "Female Role Portrayals in Print Advertising: Talking With Women About Their Perceptions and Their Preferences." *Advances in Consumer Research* 22 (1995): 753-760. Web. 15 Mar. 2015.

▮ Judge Judy
By Cody Tucholke

In this argument paper, Cody Tucholke examines public perception of judges and courtrooms based off frequent viewing of the reality television show Judge Judy. Tucholke begins by reviewing Judge Judy's successful judicial career before creating and becoming the persona "Judge Judy." This important step allows the reader to see the distinctions between a "real judge" and Judge Judy's behavior, which, unlike her qualifications, is what really is in question. As Tucholke continues his investigation, he weaves in source material that considers "real" courtroom environments and "real judges" actions. How Tucholke handles this information, whether it supports or conflicts his initial conclusion, shows the intricate relationships between reality television and the public's view of what is real.

The Case of Judge Judy V. Real Court

To anyone familiar with daytime television, *"Judge Judy"* is most certainly a household name. Possibly just as familiar is the series of statements run at the beginning of every *Judge Judy* episode: "The people are real. The cases are real. The rulings are final. This is *Judge Judy*." As this demonstrates, Judge Judy is an example of a reality television show. Many people are drawn to the show by Judge Judith Sheindlin's fiery personality and for some of the outrageous cases that go on trial. However, analysis of *Judge Judy* reveals that the show may be doing more than simply entertaining the masses. Looking at how civil court legally operates and background on Judith Sheindlin gives insight into who the Judge is and the legal foundation of her show. Observations from the show itself help to establish the general emotional atmosphere and the procedures followed for a typical case on the show. Analysis of the show against real courts displays the show's potential educational value, but criticisms of Judge Judy's personality and studies on her show's effects on the public reveal where the show falls short. All this leads to the conclusion that *Judge Judy's* portrayal of courtroom justice skews the public's knowledge of how real court works and actually affects the public's opinions on how court should work. This distortion has far reaching effects; it can affect the public's view and respect for the legal system and can affect the legal system itself in that the courts select jurors from the public.

In the United States, civil court cases revolve around "a legal dispute between two or more parties" ("Civil"). In these types of trials, the plaintiff is the one filing a complaint against the defendant. The goal of the plaintiff in these trials is to demonstrate harm that has been done to them due to the actions of the defendant and to win relief ordered by the court. Relief can take the form of a number of different things, including monetary payments or an order to cease harmful action (i.e. restraining order). Before a trial happens, the opposing sides are encouraged to settle their dispute without having to actually go to trial to save precious time and money. However, if an agreement cannot be reached, then the two sides will indeed have a date in court to receive a ruling. Most of the time, when people think of court cases, they think of the right to a trial by jury, which is where a selected group of United States citizens, called jurors, who are ideally unbiased decide the outcome of the case based on the evidence presented. However, in civil court, there are certain scenarios where it is not the best option to exercise the right to a trial by jury, and there are even times when that right does not apply[1]. In cases in small claims courts[2], small amounts of money are involved and the parties represent themselves, rather than relying on lawyers. According to Nolo[3], these types of cases "will be more complicated and harder to handle" in front of a jury versus a judge ("When"). This is because the amount of formalities involved in a jury trial is not worth going through for the small amounts of money involved in small claims courts. Normally, in a jury trial, a judge's only

---

[1] As outlined in the United States Constitution, all citizens have the right to a trial by jury in a federal civil court case. This right also applies in state civil court cases, except in what is called family court, a subdivision of state civil court that deals with issues such as divorces and child custody. According to the Federal Judicial Center's website, a state civil court case is one in which a person or organization sues another from the same state. An example would be suing for not "living up to a contract" ("Inside"). A federal civil court case is one in which the parties are from different states and the damages are over $75,000. A person, organization, or the federal government can also file a federal civil court case when federal statutes or constitutional rights may have been broken.

[2] Small claims courts are another subdivision of state civil courts.

[3] Nolo is a website that aims to give legal information to individuals and small businesses. It has an "A+" rating from the Better Business Bureau.

responsibilities are to supervise to ensure that the rules of court are followed and to hand down sentencing. In the case of what is called a bench trial, however, the judge has the added responsibility of determining the outcome based on the evidence. Bench trials ensue when both parties have waived the right to a trial by jury or when that right does not apply to the situation. In civil court, it is only necessary to prove that the defendant is more likely than not responsible for the harm done to the plaintiff.

Enter Judith Sheindlin. Judith Sheindlin is a former lawyer and real court judge. As a prosecuting attorney, she started in juvenile delinquency cases for the state of New York in 1972. After over 10 years of service there, Mayor Edward Koch appointed her to be a judge in New York City's Family Court. By 1986, she became the Supervising Judge in Manhattan. As a real judge, she heard over 20,000 cases over the years. She became well known for her reputation as a tough but fair and altogether effective judge. She was coined "[a] swift decision-maker" and was "credited with pioneering an 'open court policy,' allowing the public and the media to view her day-to-day proceedings" ("Bios"). After being impressed by an article on her by the *Los Angeles Times* in February 1993, the television show *60 Minutes* featured Judge Sheindlin on an episode. This outbreak of media attention led to the Judge being approached about a new possible television show. Judge Sheindlin retired from her occupation as a real court judge in February 1996, and on September 16, 1996, *Judge Judy* was born.

On this new show named after her, Judge Judy was to be the presiding judge. In this role, she would hear cases in bench trials brought before her by opposing parties that would normally go to a small claims court. To be on the show, both parties had to agree contractually to have their case televised and to accept the ruling and sentencing handed down by Judge Judy. The program has been a hit since its inception. As of the 2013 season, the show was ranked #1 in daytime television and the Judge was among the "100 Most Trusted Americans" according to a survey by *Reader's Digest*. This year, the show is in the middle of its 19th season. Clearly, Judith Sheindlin has made an impact on the American general public. However, has her impact overstepped the boundaries of pure entertainment? Does this show offer Americans an educational outlook on the United States legal system, at least as far as bench trials? Or does it mislead Americans in some way due to how it is run and/or its televised nature?

To begin, it may be helpful to make a few observations about *Judge Judy*. *Judge Judy* actually does a fairly good job of recreating a real court. An initial, comprehensive view of the setting at the beginning of all *Judge Judy* airings depicts many elements common to a courtroom. Tables and benches made of wood are evenly situated among the courtroom. Audience members are free to sit in rows in the back, just like the general public is free to do in many higher-level real court cases. There is a table and seating for both the plaintiff and the defendant. All of these components are situated such that they are angled toward the central focus of the judge's bench.

While *Judge Judy's* setting may provide some details on how it compares to real court, more insight can be gained from looking at specific episodes. Looking at an episode from October 31, 2014, Jennifer Watts is one of the plaintiffs depicted, and she brings a charge against the defendant, Kenneth Sorrows, that she discovered him having sex in her home. Upon first glance, there doesn't seem to be too much out of ordinary regarding this show contrasted against a real courtroom. While presenting their cases, the plaintiff and defendant do use rather informal language, but this is to be expected as neither are trained in law nor use a lawyer. Those appearing on the show do not use lawyers because *Judge Judy* is based on the small claims court model in that legal defense is not used. However, it is around seven-and-a-half minutes into the episode that some red flags start to go up. At this time, Judge Judy begins conversing with her courtroom official, Petri Hawkins Byrd[4]. While speaking to Mr. Byrd, she summarizes the argument given to her by the defendant in that he was saying he was helping a distressed woman and not having sex with her (the testimony against him clearly points to the contrary, and his story does not line up) in a mocking tone by repeating

---

[4] Mr. Byrd is a pseudo-official, in that he is supposed to represent a courtroom official whose job is to help maintain order in the court, but in practice he serves as comic relief and espouses the views of Judge Judy.

verbatim parts of what he said with an air of sarcasm and with the intent to incite laughter from the court. A strong sense of subjectivity emerges from this. Then, she conducts a normal cross-examination against Sorrows. All is normal again. However, by the end of the cross-examination, all chaos breaks loose. It begins with Mr. Byrd remarking "That's funny. I thought he was going to make something up" (Judge), which then cascades into the whole courtroom bursting into laughter. Following that up, Judge Judy asserts that Sorrows' story is one of the lamest she has ever heard. Upon further questioning, Judge Judy finally attacks Sorrows for all of the inconsistencies within his story, and when he tries to defend himself, she shouts over him by telling him to not interrupt her and simply ends the case by saying that Mr. Sorrows has insulted her intelligence. She then promptly awards Ms. Watts $3,000 in damages. Surely this is not how real courts work, right?

Perhaps it is. In an article discussing clinical law students, Steven Berenson, a professor of law at Thomas Jefferson School of Law in San Diego, examines the expectations that many of these students bring with them when they are first exposed to "poor people's courts" (family courts) upon entering law school. He states that many of these students draw their expectations from the show *Law and Order* in that they think all courtrooms are neat, orderly, and respectful. Somewhat surprisingly, Berenson asserts that, "[i] ronically, syndic-courtroom shows such as *Judge Judy*. . .may approximate the reality in poor people's courts more closely than other television and cinematic courtroom portrayals do" (367). He goes on to mention that shows like *Judge Judy*, being based off of real small claims court cases, are similar to real family courtrooms in that parties submit written submissions relating the case, answer questions from the court, and appear without lawyers; the rules of evidence don't apply; and documentary and other forms of physical evidence are kept to a minimum. Contrasting shows like *Law and Order*, there are no drawn out and dramatic opening and closing statements, nor confrontational examinations, nor jury verdicts in real family courts. Based on this information, it can clearly be argued that *Judge Judy* is both entertaining and educational, as it can accurately depict family courts. In this sense, the television viewer is getting a bonus out of watching *Judge Judy*.

However, this is not the end of the story. From here, Berenson then goes on to explain how shows like *Judge Judy* differ from real family courts, and these differences stem largely from the judges themselves. Of the television judges, he indicates that they are "aggressive, impatient, and opinionated," and that they tend toward "lengthy, often sarcastic tirades against [those appearing in court]." He claims that this is a result of television judges needing personae that attract viewers. With all this said, Judge Judy obviously has a fiery temperament for a reason. She not only needs interesting cases to have audiences coming back for more, but also a charismatic personality, so she crosses the line of a real judge to openly express herself in an effort to stay relevant and interesting. The role of a real judge is to simply ensure that courtroom protocol is followed and to decide the outcome in bench trials; Judge Judy transcends this by introducing her personality with a purpose in mind. Allowing her personality to shine through adds a dimension not normally expressed by real judges for the sake of objectivity. Judge Judy simply does this because it is good for ratings for her to let her personality be overwhelmingly present. This pattern was most certainly adopted in her transition to television to attract viewers.

Building off of this, other authors confirm the evaluations of Judge Judy offered by Berenson. In an article evaluating the various aspects of *Judge Judy*, Lawrence Friedman, a law professor at Stanford Law School, offers his take on how the Judge oversees her court. He says that her "brand of justice" is "nasty, brutish, and quick" (127). He upholds that the program is successful because of Judge Judy's "acerbic personality, the way she admonishes, insults, castigates, lectures, and humiliates" those who appear in court (127). Trending opposite of a real judge, Friedman continues to say that Judge Judy is not "wise, just, and neutral" (128). To restate this, Friedman is saying that Judge Judy intentionally breaks away from the expectations of a real judge to ensure the continued success of her show. In a different article addressing the representations of justice in the show *The People's Court* against *Judge Judy*, Steven Kohm, a faculty member in the Department of Criminal Justice at the University of Winnipeg, assesses that Judge Judy, or at least her character on the show, possesses the personal characteristics of a dynamic leader (705). Her demeanor demands reverence from people, so they respect her decisions. To take all of this into a collective whole, not only does Judge Judy have a persona that captures audiences, but her charisma also demands respect. In watching the show, people naturally trust and admire Judge Judy for her personal qualities, and her tendency to lash out at others grips audiences. Now the question arises: if Judge Judy does in fact misrepresent judges in real courtrooms, how much of an impact does this have on the general public?

It could still be argued that the educational value of *Judge Judy* outweighs the misleading personality conveyed by the Judge. Indeed, in a study on the messages sent to the public by television courtrooms, Kimberlianne Podlas, an associate professor of media studies at the University of North Carolina at Greensboro, concluded from 225 individuals reporting for jury duty that shows like *Judge Judy* do actually teach the public about the justice system, at least as far as how family court works. However, data seems to suggest that there is also much lacking from these shows. In the same study with the same 225 individuals, participants were split up into two categories based on how much television courtroom shows they watched: frequent viewers (FV) or non-viewers (NV). As displayed in Table 1 below, the FV group thought that real judges should have a more active and aggressive role in courtrooms as compared to the NV group. The FV group also showed a significantly larger percentage of those believing that silence from the judge was indicative of believing the plaintiff or defendant that was speaking. It appears these individuals may be being affected in their perceptions by the television court shows that they watch, but causality cannot be assumed, as this was merely an observational study. Observational studies cannot account for confounding variables, so a scientific experiment is necessary to determine causality.

To conclude, it is clear that people watch *Judge Judy* for a reason. Her quick wits, unabashed style, and fiery personality that are atypical of a real judge have audiences coming back for more. Perhaps this is even why people want to appear on the show. Rather than simply going to a small claims court, people would rather get their 15 minutes of fame from being verbally abused by the ever-popular Judge Judy. However, data suggests that watching shows like Judge Judy may alter public perceptions of how judges are supposed to operate within real court. These perceptions go against the dignity and justice that the courts are founded on. In the case of the study participants reporting for jury duty, one can only hope that for any of them actually named jurors in a real case that the rules of real court were clearly spelled out. However, to the general public, these perceptions, if left uncorrected, could diminish the respect that the public has for the court system and the decisions it makes. That said, when watching Judge Judy, it may be helpful to remember a few things: The people may be real. The cases may be real. The rulings may be final, but it is just a TV show.

Table 1.
Percentage of individuals from a 225-person sample responding to each prompt in the indicated fashion.

Table 1. Summary of findings	FV	NV
Judicial opinions, activity		
judges should have opinion regarding verdict	75%	48.6%
judge should make opinion "clear"	76.5%	31.58%
jurors will "look for clues" to judge's opinion	74.5%	31.58%
Aggressive, investigatory behaviors		
judge should ask questions during trial	82.5%	38.16%
judges should "be aggressive with litigants or express displeasure with their testimony"	63.76%	26.32%
Interpretation of judicial silence		
judge's silence indicates belief in litigant	73.8%	13%

Source: Podlas, Kimberlianne. "Should We Blame Judge Judy: The Messages TV Courtrooms Send Viewers." *Judicature*. 86.1 (2002): 38-43. Web. 2 Nov. 2014.

Works Cited

Berenson, Steven Keith. "Preparing Clinical Law Students for Advocacy in Poor People's Courts." *New Mexico Law Review.* 43.2 (2013): 363-396. Web. 2 Nov. 2014.

"Bios: Judge Judith Sheindlin." *Judge Judy.* Big Ticket Television, n.d. Web. 2 Nov. 2014.

"Civil Cases." *United States Courts.* Administrative Office of the U.S. Courts, n.d. Web. 2 Nov. 2014.

Friedman, Lawrence M. "Judge Judy's Justice." *Berkeley Journal of Entertainment and Sports* Law. 1.2 (2012): 125-133. Web. 2 Nov. 2014.

"Inside the Federal Courts." *Federal Judicial Center.* Federal Judicial Center, n.d. Web. 19 Nov. 2014.

Judge Judy Season 19. "Judge Judy Season 19 Full Episodes 1 October 31, 2014." Online video clip. *YouTube.* YouTube, 31 Oct 2014. Web. 5 Nov. 2014.

Kohm, Steven A. "The People's Law versus Judge Judy Justice: Two Models of Law in American Reality-Based Courtroom TV." *Law & Society Review.* 40.3 (2006): 693-728. Web. 2 Nov. 2014.

Podlas, Kimberlianne. "Should We Blame Judge Judy: The Messages TV Courtrooms Send Viewers." *Judicature.* 86.1 (2002): 38-43. Web. 2 Nov. 2014.

"When Do I Have a Right to Have My Civil Case Heard by a Jury?" *Nolo.com.* Nolo, n.d. Web. 18 Nov. 2014.

∎ Music Therapy in Alzheimer's Disease: Annotated Bibliography
By Mateo Taddeini

What follows is an annotated bibliography for research that was used in Mateo Taddeini's research paper "Music Therapy in Alzheimer's Disease: A Beginner's Approach."

Simmons-Stern, Nicholas R., et al. "Music as a Memory Enhancer in Patients with Alzheimer's Disease." *Neuropsychologia*, vol. 48, no. 10, Aug. 2010, pp. 3164–67. ScienceDirect.

The authors, researchers from the Boston University Alzheimer's Disease Center, explored the positive implications of musical mnemonics in Alzheimer Disease (AD) patients. Data was collected for the hypothesis that patients with AD and healthy older adults would respond better to song lyrics with a sung recording versus lyrics studied with a spoken recording. Patients ages 60 to 80 with AD and healthy patients in the Boston area were used in the study. Results confirmed the hypothesis proposed, and sung lyrics do provide memory enhancement in AD patients and healthy older adults. Their findings are thought to be explained by (a) the sparing of the part of the brain responsible for musical encoding and/or (b) that music increases arousal, thus improves attention and memory. This study supports my claim of the positive impacts sung music can have on AD patients that are, in this case, fully developed.

Omar, Rohani, et al. "The Cognitive Organization of Music Knowledge: A Clinical Analysis." *PMC*, vol. 133, no. 4, Apr. 2010, pp. 1200–13. NCBI.

Researchers, at the US National Library of Medicine National Institutes of Health, studied the non-verbal knowledge of music in dementia and Alzheimer's disease patients. Data was collected with relation to musical compositions, musical emotions, musical instruments, and music notation, and perceptual abilities and neuropsychological functions. It was hypothesized that dementia would create deficits in music emotion knowledge and instrument, while Alzheimer's would produce deficits of music notation and composition. A patient of 56-years of age with gradual increases in difficulty recognizing friends, progressive loss of word-finding, and naming difficulty. Results revealed that "loss of music reading skills is accompanied by a disease (Alzheimer's disease) involving the parietal lobes, whereas music reading was preserved in a disease (semantic dementia) that selectively damages the anterior temporal lobes" (Omar et al.). Similarly, to the study by Nicholas R. Simmons-Stern, this focuses on studying the implications of music therapy; however, in contrast, this study considers dementia as well.

Baird, Amee, and Séverine Samson. "Music and Dementia." *Progress in Brain Research*, vol. 217, Elsevier, 2015, pp. 207–35, http://www. sciencedirect.com/science/article/pii/S0079612314000296. ScienceDirect.

Two researchers, from the ARC Centre of Excellence in Cognition and its disorders at Macquarie University, consider the interrelationship between music and dementia (resulting in Alzheimer's disease or AD). Analysis of various research done by other researchers, even referencing Simmons-Stern (listed above). Considering all studies that attribute to research regarding memory enhancement and recovery. Their analysis suggests further research into brain mechanisms underlying musical function that should expand beyond the dementia type of AD. Comprehensively this includes information regarding various studies revolving around music and its impact on dementia patients.

Simmons-Stern, Nicholas R., Rebecca G. Deason, et al. "Music-Based Memory Enhancement in Alzheimer's Disease: Promise and Limitations." *Neuropsychologia*, vol. 50, no. 14, Dec. 2012, pp. 3295–303. ScienceDirect.

Various authors, again from the Boston University Alzheimer's Disease Center, consider the counter-statistical analysis that disproves the previous study above about sung versus spoken song lyrics. Stating that the previous study was "limited by the scope of its design" and its inability to detect false alarms and false recognition (Simmons-Stern et al.). Now, they're hypothesizing that both content and specific information would be preferentially remembered when sung in a recording versus spoken in a recording. Secondly, that stimulus condition would mediate a patient's response to studied or unstudied lyrics. Hypothesis one is supported by the results provided. In the second hypothesis results supported less false recognition; however, no difference was noted in the accurate discriminations of sung stimuli versus spoken stimuli. Clearly this journal article connects to the previous articles and contributes to conversation presented by Nicholas R. Simmons-Stern and Rohani Omar.

Geist, Mary Ellen. "The Healing Power of Music." *Brain Health and Wellness*,
Aug. 2015, https://www.aarp.org/health/brain-health/info-2015/
music-therapy-for-alzheimers.html.
A journalist, from AARP reviewing Brain Health and Wellness, strives to summarize the findings across America that support the idea that music works to improve mood of these suffering from neurodegenerative diseases. Not only this, but that it can also boost cognitive skills and reduce the necessity for antipsychotic drugs. Further, this considers the views of neurologists, including Oliver Sacks and Jane Flinn, and a musical therapist, Connie Tomaino. This review focuses on bringing together some ideologies behind memory enhancement and sharing stories regarding its success. Similarly, to the research studies presented above are providing (Nicholas R. Simmons-Stern et al.) or bringing together (Rohani Omar et al.) previous research in order to contribute to the conversation.

News, CBS. "Using Music to Help Unlock Alzheimer's Patients' Memories."
CBS Evening News, CBS, 16 Aug. 2017, https://www.cbsnews.com/
news/using-music-to-help-unlock-alzheimers-patients-memories/.

Dr. John LePook reviews how the music and memory program, treated by social worker Dan Cohen, has introduced music as a treatment for Alzheimer's. In Cobble Hill Health Center in Brooklyn headphone music was provided to all patients, gradually, however, this spread to over 4,500 sites. By providing music in nursing homes to AD patients, they are able to connect emotionally. Dr. LePook says, "Since the music we love is really tied to our emotional system, and our emotional system is still very much intact, that's what we're connecting and that's what still works". This video demonstrates the application of music therapy for Alzheimer's patients within certain boundaries that are now expanding.

Belluck, Pam. *What Is Alzheimer's Disease?* 30 Apr. 2016, https://www.nytimes. com/2016/05/02/science/what-is-alzheimers-disease html.
Author, Pan Belluck, defines the term Alzheimer's disease and gives meaning to the various diagnoses, causes, preventions, and treatments, of the disease. This overview provides a general audience with the ability to effectively understanding how research in Alzheimer's disease may actually be done. Further, this connects to developing the overall idea of the research paper by bringing out key terminology and treatments already in place, in order to provide an effective case for the importance of what the research paper will attempt to tackle. Thus, this newspaper article provides a comprehensive summary item that can be used for background information.

▌Fish Can't Climb

By Anaa Jibicho

In "Fish Can't Climb," Anaa Jibicho argues for the importance of African-Americans choosing to become teachers in American schools. After documenting and explaining some of the obstacles that might dissuade African-Americans from the teaching profession, Jibicho highlights the potential transformative impacts that more African-American teachers could have on students and society more broadly. In this way, the essay invites readers to think critically about societal challenges and possible solutions, encouraging a broad audience to reflect on how career choices position each of us within much larger and longer historical legacies.

Fish Can't Climb

Lyle Dandridge always had a love for teaching, but after graduating from University of Illinois with a BS in Biology, Dandridge took a year off and worked as a microbiologist researcher to see if he still had that passion. During this time that he had a chance to work with an African-American student: Keenan Dandridge was aware that Keenan was in a hard spot in his life, his father and older brother had recently been locked up on drug charges and Keenan was heading towards that avenue. Dandridge recalls a conversation between them. "Yo, Mr. D," voiced Keenan', "you're a scientist?" Bewildered, Mr. D replied, "yeah, I'm a scientist." "I could be a scientist?" asked the youngin' anxiously. "No doubt, of course," Mr. D responded confidently. "Word," Keenan rejoiced, "that's what I'm gonna do" (Dandridge). You see, Black teachers have lots of influence on black students: they develop trust and rapport, they have high expectation of them, and they serve as an example of how to overcome challenges and become successful. Due to the shortage of African-American teachers, prospective African-American teachers have an obligation to become teachers.

Many critics says that some prospective black teachers turn away from teaching because of their genuine stance that educational equality is a function of who holds the power in the classroom. Sometime after the so though of success of Brown v.s. Board of Education began the integration of schools. It wasn't integration in a sense that black students were put into white schools and white students into black schools. No. Many black institutions were closed down and over 40,000 black teachers lost their jobs (Evans). Black students were put into white institutions with no teachers that resemble their melanin. These institutions weren't reformed so that they could work for both the white students and the black students, no, it was left as it was; benefiting the white students. Research done by two scientists at Vanderbilt University, Jason Grissom and Christopher Redding say, " [today] two students who are similar on math and reading achievement in elementary school, a White student and a Black student, that White student is still more than two times as likely to be receiving gifted services as that Black student." The researchers go on to conclude, "teachers play a big role... they encourage them, they recommend them... the answer here lies with not who the child is but who the child's teacher is," (Grissom). White teachers have lower expectations than black teachers for the same black students (DeRuy). There's then this talk about achievement gaps. Of course you'll have achievement gaps if the standard is measured on the scales of how much one aligns with the white institutions. As Dandridge remarked, "I know kids that aren't proficient in the english grammar, but can put some rhymes together, but there isn't much classes on usage of original analogies and metaphors. That's english mastery too" (Dandridge). The debate about achievement gaps is like judging a fish by it's ability to climb a tree. The underlying problem is that the schools systems in the united states just isn't equipped for black students to succeed. Why should one teach in a system that isn't made for them?

Although true and reasonable to conclude that schools systems in the united states isn't made for black people, I find it rather foolish to use that as a reason for African-American prospective teacher not to become a teacher. During the abolitionist era, there were many notable abolitionists, and they weren't all black. In fact, there were many white abolitionists. There were a great deal of white abolitionists that were buying black slaves and liberating them (Thatcher). They didn't just stay in the shadows and complain about the brutal system of slavery, they realised the immortality of it and did the best they were capable of in not advancing such a system. They became the change they wanted to see.

Some tougher skeptics will argue that those abolitionists weren't helping the struggle against slavery, they were in fact fueling it. Although they were buying the slaves and liberating them, they were still buying the slaves. They were investing in the slave trade despite their efforts to fight against it. So if African-American teachers continue teaching in a school system that isn't made for African-Americans, they're perpetuating the facade that the school systems is working for African-Americans, when in reality, it is not.

This again, is a fair point, but fails to overlook the fact that the abolitionists goal of ending slavery succeeded. It would not have happened if it wasn't for their efforts that sustained the anti-slavery movement. The abolitionists weren't just fighting against the slave owners. There was a silent majority that was on the fence about slavery, but they would not speak up because no one else is. So in order to end slavery, the abolitionists had to model to the silent majority that there are other white people that are freeing slaves. They had to inspire them. This liberating of the slaves evoked more and more of the morals of the slave owners into freeing their slaves. As this movement continued, it led to the Civil war and the liberation of all slaves. Imagine what would have happened if the few white prospective abolitionists would have thought that, although the slavery system was a reprehensible thing, they won't become abolitionists because the system just wasn't made for an anti-slavery movement. Slavery would have kept happening for a lot longer. Therefore, Prospective African-American teachers shouldn't let the fact that school systems wasn't made for black people stop them from entering the school system. There's a silent majority today in regards to the school system, many people don't know how unfair it is. If more African-American teachers get into the school systems and educated student of all likes about the injustice of the school systems, there are bound to be school reforms that make the school systems work for everyone.

The burden of being a black teacher: Black tax. Getting black professionals into teaching is hard, but that's just half the battle for solving the scarcity of black teachers. The other part is keeping teachers in the classroom once they're there. At a time in which we need more black teachers, it's shown that more black teachers leave the profession than any other race. One in five black teachers leave that profession to be exact (Di-Carlo). Many leave because of their frustration in being "pigeonholed." Pigeonholed, is the equivalent of the black tax in the education system. You know, the idea that Black people have to work and perform regular tasks twice as well as White people. Black teachers report that they feel like a disciplinary figure because too many black disruptive students are placed in their classes at the same time because other teachers believe that, "if somebody can handle them, it's this dude that looks like them." Sure, this allows the black teachers to interact more with the black students, but it is unmanageable and frustrating because too many undisciplined students are put into one class.

I find this to be a very honest and fair rationale, but, nonetheless, not a satisfying reason to leave a teaching position. If having more black teachers shows to improve a black student's experience within school, there would be less black students who are disruptive. If there less disruptive black students then it's safe to assume that the frustration of the black tax in schools would be lower, or in existent. And as more black teachers enter the system, there would be less black tax. Black teachers in schools serve as role models for black students, if some black teachers leave from their frustration of the black tax, more burden falls onto other black teachers who now have more disruptive black students in their classes, thus winding them down to leave teaching also. For those reasons, prospective black teachers have an obligation to other black teachers and black students to become teachers.

A large portion of a youngster's time is spent in a classroom learning the fundamentals of life as they prepare to go out into the world. So much time is spent with teachers allowing students to create bonds that are life-changing. For a significant number of us, teachers influenced college to appear to be possible and our dreams attainable. Majority of teachers in this nation are white at a time in which minority students are the majority within classrooms, however, they experience considerable difficulties finding an educator that looks like them and can relate to their own issues (DeRuy). There's an incredible need for black teachers in the classrooms. There are many benefits of having black teachers, and not just for black students.

For white students, black teacher counters their biases. Black teachers are black excellence embodied, and when our black students see them in a classroom, they see that the sky's the limit.

Mr. D doesn't know if Keenan went on to become a scientist, but he says it doesn't matter. That interaction was enough to make him realize "how much power it is for people to see an educated black man." I asked Dandridge if that experience made him feel a sense of obligation to become a teacher, "yeah. I did. I did see that as an obligation. I knew what I was going to do with my life now." Dandridge went on to become a teacher. He has an impact on kid's lives everyday. He doesn't plan to leave teaching anytime soon either. Dandridge hopes to continue connecting to the diverse student population, especially black students. Dandridge always wanted to become a teacher, but he went through a phase in his life that made him question those possibilities (Dandridge). This is in contrast to Malcolm X's concept of the House Negro and the Field Negro: this shows how historically, the black middle class has compromised the interest of black people as whole to advance their own interest which was inextricably tied to the perpetuation of the white power structure (X). There sure are many reasonable obstacles and dilemmas in becoming a black teacher, but the potential impact of black teachers is far greater than ever. Black men and women who are on the fence on becoming teachers should step up to the plate and become the role models that they needed when they were younger. Prospective black teachers have an obligation to become teachers.

Works Cited

Dandridge, Lyle. Personal Interview. 22 Nov. 2017.

DeRuy, Emily. "White Teachers Expect Less Than Black Teachers From Black Students." *The Atlantic*, Atlantic Media Company, 1 Apr. 2016, www. theatlantic.com/education/archive/2016/04/white-teachers-expect-less-than-black-teachers-from-black-students/476307/.

Di Carlo, Mathew. "Update On Teacher Turnover In The U.S." *Shanker Institute*, 23 Feb. 2015, www.shankerinstitute.org/blog/update-teacher-turnover-us.

Evans, Brian R, and Jacqueline Leonard. "Recruiting and Retaining Black Teachers to Work in Urban Schools." *SAGE Open*, www.journals. sagepub.com/doi/abs/10.1177/2158244013502989.

Grissom, Jason, and Christopher Redding. "Discretion and Disproportionality: Explaining the Underrepresentation of High-Achieving Students of Color in Gifted Programs." *American Educational Research Association*, journals.sagepub.com/doi/abs/10.1177/2332858415622175

Thatcher, B. B. *American Colonization Society*. North American Review, 1832.

X, Malcolm. "Message to Grassroots." Malcolm X. 10 Oct. 1963, teachingamericanhistory.org/library/index.asp?document=1145.

∎ All My Brown

By Gayatri Lakshmi Narayanan

Gayatri Lakshmi Narayanan's research paper explores, through the use of empirical evidence and scholarly studies, the racial biases and discrimination that develops around the color brown. It is a paper of strong senses and vivid scenes that allow the reader to be in that kitchen, that doctor's office, and that science lab reading and watching as Narayanan works through what it means to be brown. As much a research paper on racial disparities as it is personal narrative on identity, "All My Brown" is fluidly weaved through a logical structure and unified under a steady voice. Most impressive is Narayanan's collected set of empirical evidence that shows how such data compounds, building over time to reveal the causes and effects of how things come to be.

All My Brown

Introduction

My box of crayons usually had one colour that looked brand new in comparison to the stubs that used to be other colours. As a child, I hated using brown in art class. Perhaps it reminded me of my own skin colour, and the conflict of always having used the peach colour pencils to shade humans in art class in school. I did not know then of brown to be the colour of beautiful things, like trees, mud, and food. Interestingly, the appearance of the term 'brown' in child-directed speech is significantly less than other colour terms, and children have been found to prefer the colour brown significantly less than basic colours. This means that colour preference may be linked to the language of colour (1). The absence of interaction between the colour and our words results in a void about the qualities we prescribe to brown. As a result, in talking about our own skins, the question of who is brown and what shade of brown is both intimate and uncomfortable.

Brown covers my body and surrounds me, in everything I see. It simmers in the pressure cooker. It clumps around the spinach plants. It climbs and falls from the trees. It melts between holding hands. Brown is a reservoir of memory and emotion. In this paper, I will be dipping into the colour to generate sensory experiences that can fill the body of a scientific research paper.

Andrew Solomon says, "Forge meaning. Build identity. Identity involves entering a community to draw strength from that community, and to give strength there, too. It involves substituting "and" for "but"..." My mother tells me not to label myself as anything. I find Mr. Solomon's approach richer.

I am brown and I am here. I am brown *and* I am *here*.

Dal Makhani and *Pongal*

Brown celebrates the sweet, tangy, sticky, melting with butter, spicy, and wholesome. It is the primary colour in our food. My mother only buys unprocessed, organic ingredients. We joke at home that everything is brown-the rice, the eggs, the sugar. *Amma* cooks her ingredients into every shade of brown.

Dal makhani is rich, slightly sweet, creamy and savoury bliss in a copper pot that is meant to drip from a buttery piece of *naan*[1]. Restaurant-made dal makhani has a distinct colour. It is shiny, bordering on almost orange. When *Amma* made it at home, it was served in little steel bowls into which I dipped a hot piece of *roti*. The roti was warm, and dotted with darker brown patches where it had been burnt a little. The dal[2] made at home was darker than in the restaurants. It tasted earthier.

Pongal is my favourite sweet dish. My mother makes it for our new year celebration, which comes every spring. We always start our meals with a little bit of the sweet dish, and there is no joy like picking up the grains of Pongal between my fingers, tasting their sweetness in my mouth, and biting into a plump raisin.

---

1 Naan and roti are types of Indian breads that are eaten with lentils or vegetables
2 Dal refers to lentils

Methods

Amma washed the dal and placed it in the big round steel bowl. The beans were wet, shiny, and dark brown. The bowl was filled with warm water in which the dal soaked for three hours. The white kitchen light hit the wet beans and the steel container, reflecting light everywhere. An eager child walked into the kitchen and hovered over the bowl. The water was drained and dal washed again. Amma added five cups of water, two tablespoons of ghee, salt and ginger-garlic paste to the pressure cooker container. The dal was cooked for another thirty minutes. The brown swelled and suddenly gained taste. To the dal in the cooker, *Amma* added tomato puree, kasoori methi, garam masala, jaiphal powder[3], and butter. The tomato would give the dal its shine and reddish earthy undertone. The dal simmered for thirty minutes. *Amma* stirred it occasionally. The dal was transferred to a wok. By this time, at least one child had to be told to vacate the wooden swing in front of the television and get back to studying before dinner was served. To the dal, *Amma* added milk mixed with cream. This made the gorgeous brown even richer and creamier. *Amma* mixed the dal well and let it simmer to develop the colour and smoothness. She then began rolling out the *rotis* and calling for her children to come set the table.

To make the Pongal, *Amma* cooked the rice, lentils and milk until they formed a soft, pulpy mass. Then, over a low flame, she added the molasses. Molasses is sold as a cylindrical block that is cut with a knife into shavings to be powdered and mixed in the dish. The rice-milk mixture welcomed the dark golden-brown sugar as *Amma* stirred and turned over the mixture in the pan multiple times to prevent it from sticking and leaving stubborn burnt brown marks. The rice, milk and sugars were cooked until the *Pongal* became sticky.

Cashew nuts, raisins, and nutmeg were fried and added to the *Pongal*. Each one studded the *Pongal* with a different edible brown. The cashew nuts were smooth and light brown, raisins wrinkly, sweet, juicy, and the spicy-sweet nutmeg was the colour of caramel. A lot of clarified butter was added in the end to bind all the brown together and coat every grain, nut, and raisin with the tastiest glow.

---

3 Kasoori methi, garam masala and jalphal powder are spices and seasonings

Results

Mayank left the rich brown flavours of home for Paris, where he studies at Le Cordon Bleu. Last week, he cut a nerve and an artery in an accident in the kitchen. When he was receiving stiches for his cuts, his blood spurted out of the cut artery. The doctors told him he had HIV based on his blood, and the chestnut brown of his skin. He believed he had HIV for a week. His eyes are green, flecked with brown- hazel. As his best friend from middle school, I have had the privilege of hiding with him from the girls in school who were especially attracted to the colours of his eyes. It hurts to know that those eyes held fear. Yesterday, he received his secondary results for an HIV test. They were negative.

Brown packages hold damaged goods. There is a large body of scientific study that points to the correlation between racial bias and lower quality of healthcare.

Of course, in psychiatry we see this [discrimination]. One area we see is in terms of diagnosis. Patients are inappropriately diagnosed and medications prescribed for the patients. We see errors in that. Minority patients will often be diagnosed inappropriately as being schizophrenic. (African-American physician) (2)

It is an unstable layer at the interface of many interactions. So, I gently poured the sulphuric acid down the sides of the test tube. I held the tube steady and took in a slight breath. My eyes lit up and I called for my Chemistry teacher, Mr. Vasu. He stood in front of the test tube I was holding up, peering into it with the biggest smile on his face. The result of the test was clear. The appearance of the brown ring at the interface of the sample and the sulphuric acid confirmed the presence of nitrate ions in the sample being tested. I held the tube carefully to keep the brown layer from decomposing, and I was no longer the clumsiest chemistry student in my grade.

Conclusion

Brown is a personal history, a method, a cause, and a result. My copper-golden skin, that I am said to have inherited from my grandfather, flows into the hands of a dear friend; his brown- flecked eyes hold magic. I consume food harvested from the mud, that my mother cooks into a swollen, delicious mix of browns. And all these browns culminate in the delicate balance of two liquids in a test tube, indicative of our larger experiment. From one skin to another, the brown flows in and out of our bodies. Its beauty lies in its instability, how quickly it deepens and darkens over the fire, the grief it has brought collectives of people, and finally, in this acceptance.

I am brown and I am here. I am brown *and* I am *here*.

References

1. N. J. Pitchford, K. T. Mullen, The role of perception, language, and preference in the developmental acquisition of basic color terms. *J. Exp. Child Psychol.* 90, 275–302 (2005).

2. B. D. Smedley, A. Y. Stith, A. R. Nelson, *Unequal Treatment: Confronting Racial and Ethnic Disparities in Health Care* (2002), vol. 94.

∎ Escaping the Cycle: A Critical Inquiry into Native American Poverty and its Causes, with a Comparison into Cultural and Traditional Values, Followed by an Analysis and Solutions

By Nathaniel Smith

In this well-researched essay, Nathaniel takes on the social and political disenfranchisement of Native American populations. He presents a compelling case about the lack of attention paid to Native Americans in poverty, and offers solutions based on healthcare, education, land development, and sovereignty. Nathaniel synthesizes several arguments in order to successfully make his case for social, cultural, and political equity for Native American populations.

Escaping the Cycle: A Critical Inquiry into Native American Poverty and its Causes, with a Comparison into Cultural and Traditional Values, Followed by an Analysis and Solutions

"From poverty of a man, even his friends heed not his words. His power is laughed at; none desire his acquaintance, nor speaks to him with respect. Truly poverty is the sixth great sin." – Charudatta, "Mricchakatika" 2nd Century B.C.E. play by Sudrakah

"We fought a war on poverty and poverty won." – Ronald Reagan, 1987

"Today, a vicious cycle of poverty, criminality, and incarceration traps too many Americans and weakens too many communities..." – Eric Holder, 2013

Poverty among Native Americans has been present for as long as reservations themselves. As part of the decision rendered by the Supreme Court under *Cherokee Nation v. Georgia,* John Marshall wrote: "[M]eanwhile, they are in a state of pupilage. Their relations to the United States resemble that of a ward to his guardian."[4] While this decision came 182 years ago, its derisive attitude towards another race is highlighted in the key words "pupilage" and "ward;" these words imply a sense of subservience and, in my opinion, classify

---

1 Cherokee Nation v. Georgia, 1831

Native peoples as subhuman. The word that best describes this mindset is racist. The Australian Human Rights Commission defines racism as "a set of beliefs, often complex, that asserts the natural superiority of one group over another, and which is often used to justify differential treatment and social positions."[5] Racism directed towards Native Americans has persisted to the modern day: Native Americans consistently earn less, have worse health, live on land that goes undeveloped because banks are unwilling to provide loans, have lower levels of educational attainment, and higher incarceration rates. Although these statements appear to be supported by statistics, they are gross simplifications of the issue at hand.

This simplification is also present in the issue of poverty. The prevailing stereotype about poor people is that they are lazy, or that they have no "habits for working" for pay "unless it's illegal," a statement made by Republican Presidential candidate Newt Gingrich in December 2011.[3] That a person who served as Speaker of the House of Representatives as recently as 1999 not only acknowledges this stereotype (which can be directly linked to any of the stereotypes above), but outright embraces it, demonstrates that there needs to be a culture of change in America and around the world.

Escaping the poverty cycle is, and has been since the rise of civilization, a difficult task indeed. According to a report by the Pew Charitable Trusts released in November 2013, of the approximately 60 million Americans born into the bottom quintile of the "income ladder," 70% do not emerge above the 40th percentile, a staggering statistic that is less pronounced for white Americans than any other race.[4] This stands in stark contrast to the American Dream: hard work and determination can overcome birthright, especially for those not born as American citizens. Andrew Carnegie and Warren Buffett stand as the prime examples supporters of objectivism[5], a philosophy brought

---

2 Australian Human Rights Commission
3 CBS News, Dec. 1, 2011
4 Pew Charitable Trusts, Nov. 2013
5 Objectivism, according to Rand's] appendix of Atlas Shrugged, is "the concept of man as a heroic being with his own happiness as the moral pursuit of his life, with productive achievement as his noblest activity, and reason as his absolute."

to the forefront by author Ayn Rand, point to when asked if the American Dream still holds any ballast. Living in poverty is the exact opposite of the American Dream, and is often a crucial reason for immigrate to the United States; how, then, can it be achieved if one still lives in poverty upon becoming an American?

What is omitted from this argument is that the economic ladder is inherently biased. Those with the upper hand at the beginning often maintain this advantage. In a simplification of the issue, those with the best weapons and the best literacy will almost always be at the top, and subjugate those without such advantages.[6] Of the 30 richest individuals in American history, not a single one is female or a non-Caucasian male.[7] Among Forbes' 50 Richest Americans today, there is a slightly greater parity, although the WASP still holds sway: there are seven females listed, although each one has inherited a great deal of their wealth. There are two minorities among the top fifty: Patrick Soon Shiong and Pierre Omidyar, each of whom achieved his wealth by his own work.[8] Economic analysts may still believe that America is a land of opportunity and equality, but the top of the ladder clearly suggests otherwise.

The second major issue which I feel I must address is the issue of sovereignty rights. This idea is that Native Americans, by virtue of their heritage, are due lands belonging to their ancestors and that they should not be subject to the laws of the United States. This is where reservations become a favorable outcome. Inhabitants are subject to the laws of the reservation. Where this becomes an issue is when, excluding Puerto Rico, nine of the eleven poorest counties by median income, none of which exceed $9,251 per capita, have a majority Native American population.[9] A large proportion of the reservation population receives welfare from the U.S. government, although it is treated as aid to a foreign nation. When Native Americans try

---

6 Note: I do realize the irony in using a simplification of the issue, but the idea of literacy and warfare as the driving factors behind the rise to power of the white, Anglo-Saxon Protestant, straight, Upper Class male could easily fill an entire paper by itself and that is not the topic on which I am focusing.
7 NYTimes.com, July 2007
8 Forbes 400, as of Sept. 2013
9 U.S. Census Bureau

to move off the reservation and compete for jobs, many find that they are at a disadvantage because of their background. A solution has yet to be found which strikes a balance between legal independence from the United State and support from the U.S. government to enable American Indians to be more competitive in the market. By the end of this essay, I hope to establish a set of logical solutions that accomplishes this goal.

Part I: Reservations

Among the issues at the core of the problem is that of health and healthcare. Several reservations boast the highest rates of diabetes and heart disease, among many others, as well as a life expectancy equivalent to that of Guinea-Bissau, or the sixth lowest expectancy in the world.[1010] The United States has an average life expectancy of 79 years, or 29 years more than a reservation technically within its borders.[11] The Pine Ridge Reservation of the Oglala Sioux tribe in Shannon County, South Dakota exemplifies this disparity. In 2004, the most recent date for which accurate data is available, 71.9% of Native Americans were overweight or obese (compare to 66.3% for all Americans).[12,13] Heart disease and diabetes occur at 3 times the national rate. Infant mortality is 2.34 times the national level. Deaths relating to alcohol were nearly 14 times, diabetes six times, heart disease 1.7 times, and suicide 3.1 times the national average.[14] For fiscal year 2009, only $1,132 was spent on health care per capita on the reservation, compared to $3,261 for the national average.[15]

Another indication of reservation poverty is the crisis in education. In 2000, only 27.2% of the population of Pine Ridge earned a high school degree. Only 8% proceeded to earn an Associate degree and 5.7% a Bachelor's degree. One in 33 inhabitants earned a Master's or Professional degree.[16] The national averages for these numbers were: 28.6% earned a high school degree,

10 WHO, 2011
11 Ibid
12 "Oglala Lakota College Case Statement," 2012
13 CDC, 2009
14 "Oglala Lakota College Case Statement," 2012
15 Ibid
16 "Pine Ridge Indian Reservation Population and Housing," 2009

6.3% an Associate degree, 15.5% a Bachelor's degree and 8.9% a Master's or Professional degree.[17] Like with any other group, a college degree means a considerable amount of more money. For Native Americans, each of the median incomes for four major educational attainment levels (No high school diploma, High school diploma without college, Some college but no degree, and a Bachelor's degree or higher) was lower than the median income for the United States as a whole. The table below is from the Journal of Multicultural, Gender, and Minority Studies, adjusted to 2013 levels:[18,19]

	U.S. Population	American Indians	Percent Difference
All educational levels	$40,868.06	$26,546.18	-54.0%
Less than a high school diploma	$17,003.68	$12.234.75	-38.98%
High school graduates, no college	$28,816.42	$24,066.48	-19.7%
Some college, no degree	$36,848.27	$30,158.30	-22.2%
Bachelor's degree or higher	$66,586.12	$52,513.95	-26.8%
Source: U.S. Census Bureau 2006. Figures include individuals with no earnings. IHEP, 2007, p. 26			

These data show that, even with an equivalent education, Native Americans are earning less money than their counterparts. In 1999, admittedly a date earlier than I would like, the poorest reservation had a median income of $4,043 (equivalent of $5,682.26 in 2013) and the highest had a median income of $17,436 (equal to $24,505.53 in 2013).[20] The poverty line in America in 2013 is $23,492 for a family of four.[21]

One school of thought, primarily composed of financial experts, believes that the issue is not in health issues or lower levels of higher education. A 2011 Forbes article discusses the issue of property rights. John Koppisch writes that as "[t]he vast majority of land on reservations is held communally...Native Americans...can't use the money as collateral" in

---

17 2000 U.S. Census
18 Harrington and Hunt, 2008
19 These numbers are for all Native Americans, not just those living in reservation or urban settings.
20 Anderson, 2011
21 CNN Money, Sept. 2013

order "to establish credit and borrow money..."[22] This would suggest that interactions with non-tribal lending agencies are almost counterproductive, as many banks are unwilling to loan money when they have no collateral. Land surrounding the reservations is of the same or lower potential, but because of development by private landowners (usually Caucasian), this land is of much higher value. Without investment, it is difficult for Native Americans to achieve equality financially, which in turn makes it difficult to achieve equality in other sectors. This stands in contrast to the long-held belief that when Indians were relocated to reservations, they were moved to lands that were barren. Although development of land arose long after relocation began, development for Native Americans has yet to occur, aside from casinos and the like, which have not demonstrated to effectively benefit Native Americans, according to a report by Dwanna Robertson of Indian Country Today Media Network.[23]

As with most other issues, or "symptoms" (a term to which Koppisch relegates all non-purely fiscal matters), the Pine Ridge Reservation presents a stark example of this scenario. Supported by a research grant from the Graduate School of Colorado State University, Dr. Kathleen Pickering and Dr. David Mushinski conducted research at Pine Ridge concluding in 1999. In their report, Drs. Pickering and Mushinski found conditions similar to what Koppisch described twelve years later: "Currently there are no banks within the boundaries of the Reservation, which is equivalent in size to the state of Connecticut and has a population of 11,000 to 35,000 residents."[24] In the United States, there is one bank for every 54,254 persons and one bank per 40.8 sq. miles.[25] By comparison, Sierra Leone, where 76.08% lives below the world poverty line of $2 PPP, has one bank for every 33,000 persons and one bank per 153.88 sq. miles.[26] While comparing an area of the United States to a sub-Saharan country may seem dramatic or sensational, it is a comparison

---

22 "Why are Indian reservations so poor? A look at the bottom 1%" Forbes, 12/13/2011.
23 "The Myth of Indian Casino Riches" Indian Country Today Media Network, 6/23/2012
24 Pickering and Mushinski, pg. 2
25 Calculated using statistics from Google and Federal Reserve Bank of St.
26 World Bank, 2011

that must be made. How can we, a nation that prides itself on helping smaller nations in need, feel content or ignore a situation where, in 1998, 66% of reservation inhabitants lived below the poverty line? Although this rate has fallen to 53.5% by 2011, that number is still 3.56 times the national average.[27,28] These data are a signifier that, while maintaining tradition may be a morally and emotionally action, it is not an economically viable one, especially in a world where income disparity is at its greatest in decades, an issue that prompted Zhu Min, special adviser to the International Monetary Fund, to say that "the increase in inequality is the most serious challenge for the world."[29]

Part II: Urban Areas

While the situation is more pronounced on reservations, the crisis of American Indian poverty in urban areas is nearly as significant. Cities, and especially cities in America, are supposed to be a great opportunity for social mobility. Chinese immigrants arriving in San Francisco in the nineteenth and early twentieth centuries called it gum saan, or Gold Mountain.[30] For many Native Americans, cities like Los Angeles, Phoenix, Minneapolis, New York, Albuquerque, and, incidentally, San Francisco, cities remain their gum saan. They could escape the cycle of poverty that ensnared their family and reservation for decades and rise in the ranks. Diane Humetewa, a nominee for the federal judgeship in Arizona by President Obama and a Hopi Indian, was born in Phoenix and is the first Native American woman, and third Native American ever, to be nominated for a federal judgeship, should act as a role model in coming years.[31] Over seventy percent of Native Americans live in urban areas (far lower than any other major racial group), but few have reaped the benefits of increased median income: for 2000, the median per-capita income for all urban Americans was $22,736, or $30,835.67 in 2013.

---

27 Pickering and Mushinski, pg. 7
28 U.S. Census Bureau
29 The Telegraph, Jan. 2011
30 The Chinese Exclusion Era: Conflict and Compromise on Gold Mountain
31 CBS News, Sept. 20, 2013

For urban Native Americans, the respective numbers are $15,312 in 2000, or $20,766.88, still below the poverty rate.[32,33] In Chicago, Houston, New York City, Oklahoma City, Denver, Tucson, and Phoenix, the poverty rate for Native Americans is over 25 percent, a number that increases in the under-18 group.[34] For urban areas as a whole, this total is 26 percent; on reservations, it increases to 39% of the population.[35]

The issues present on reservations, notably those of health and education, are present in urban areas. These are joined by the presence of Native American gangs and a homelessness rate that is far beyond the average for all other races. According to the National Coalition for the Homeless, 8% of all homeless people are Native American "compared to 1% of the general population."[36] Forty-one percent of the homeless population is white (76% of general population), forty percent African-American (11% general population), and eleven percent for Hispanic (9% of the general population).[37]

While gangs are a presence on many reservations, ranging from Oklahoma to Wisconsin to the Dakotas, the situation is worsened in cities where contact with other gangs, especially of other races, leads to increased conflict. This increased conflict leads to a need for more protection, which inevitably leads to greater gang participation. Coupled with unemployment, this leads to high levels of alcoholism and drug use. Educational attainment levels are similar to those on reservations. Thus, the potential that the cities represented is lost on many Native Americans.

Part III: Analysis

Social mobility in the United States has become a thing of the past. While role models may very well be positive indicators of things to come, oftentimes they are, to their contemporaries at the very least, exceptions to the rule, rather than the norm. According to U.S. Census Bureau data,

32 Harvard, The State of the Native Nations, 2007
33 BLS CPI Inflation Calculator
34 New York Times, Apr. 14, 2013
35 Harvard
36 National Coalition for the Homeless, July 2009
37 Ibid

approximately 545 million people have lived in the United States since 1790.[38][38] Of those 545,000,000, only 43 have been elected President of the United States. That equates to a 0.0000000789% chance that any American will be elected President. However, these statistics do not tell the whole story. There has been one Catholic president, zero non-Christian presidents, one non-white President, and zero female presidents. This shows that people we lionize are atypical of what not only Americans, but people around the world, can accomplish in their lifetimes.

While this train of thought may seem tangential, it is pertinent to my main argument. With little to no voice in national politics, Native Americans see fewer opportunities for progress than any other minority. Not since the early 1970s have Native American rights grabbed the attention of the American populace. Each President since, oddly enough, Richard Nixon[39] has publicly supported Native American rights but, aside from a few pieces of legislation regarding repatriation (return of ancestral artifacts) rights, little progress has been made inside the Beltway.

This lack of progress can be partially attributed to the conditions faced by Native Americans in urban areas. Because of their status as sovereign states, tribes living on reservations *technically* have no voice in American politics, even if tribal members were born off the reservation. Thus, it is up to urban American Indians to "pick up the slack," to use the vernacular. In response to the Civil Rights Movement, but not affiliated with it, the Native American sovereignty movement of the late 1960s and early 1970s had the potential to achieve the success experienced by black Americans. It had all the makings of a social movement: dynamic young leaders from urban areas (including Dennis Banks, Clyde Bellecourt, and Russell Means, among many others), support in the White House (Leonard Garment, Barbara Kilberg, and Brad Patterson, as well as Pres. Nixon to a lesser extent, if only because of the Vietnam War), support from the media, and support from celebrities (Marlon Brando's refusal

---

38 "How Many Americans Have There Been?"
39 Although not particularly if you examine his personal history more closely. For more information, please watch http://www.youtube.com/watch?v=iCKf-VonsY4

to accept his award for *The Godfather* because of the poor treatment of Native Americans). However, as the 1970s shifted the focus from achieving social equity to achieving economic equity, Native Americans have yet to catch up.

Another element is the resounding racism. Like any minority, Native Americans face racism in the social, economic, and political sectors. Among all Native Americans in 2000, 52.3 of 1,000 experienced some form of violence in the past year, 53.4% higher than that of any other race.[40] In a2001 report, the Department of Justice said that "one in 10 racially motivated bias incidents targeted Native Americans."[41] A famous incident occurred in 1975, when Leonard Peltier, an Anishinabe-Lakota member of the American Indian Movement, a radical group similar to the Black Panthers, allegedly shot and killed two white FBI agents on the Pine Ridge Reservation. Peltier was convicted of their murder and sentenced to two consecutive life sentences. However, an examination of evidence and testimony following the trial suggested that the case against Peltier was racially motivated and Peltier was a believable scapegoat, due to his history of issues with crime. Peltier has remained in federal prison since his conviction and each appeal has failed.

Part IV: Conclusion

As I am not a Native American, these solutions may seem inappropriate to someone who has experienced the problems detailed above. However, based on my research, what follows are solutions that I believe may be viable, while maintaining elements of tradition and sovereignty.

Health: I believe that, in addition to the Indian Health Service, the United States government should provide low-cost healthcare to Native Americans that matches or exceeds the best healthcare available to most Americans. A prime example for this would be that of Canada and the First Nations. Because of treaties signed with tribal leaders that enabled them to use their land and resources, Canada has allowed tribal members to use healthcare resources for free, as if they were Canadian citizens. This might not be a terribly logical

40 Indianz.com, Apr. 2002
41 Indianz.com, Oct. 2001

solution at the moment, with the Affordable Healthcare Act freezing up progress in Washington, but I believe that if it works in Canada, then there is no reason why it should not work in the United States. I believe that this solution would lower the rates of alcoholism, teenage pregnancy, diabetes, obesity, drug use, and suicide among Native Americans. I am not suggesting a reliance on U.S. hospitals and healthcare, but merely have it remain a viable and affordable option.

Education: A previous "solution" to the "problem" of Native education were off-reservation boarding schools, popularized by Richard Pratt, who was proud to say that his boarding school in Carlisle, Pennsylvania "Killed the Indian in him, and Saved the White man in him." Obviously, assimilation is not a viable solution as I seek to preserve and expand sovereignty in each of these solutions. Thus, I think that Native Americans should receive heavily subsidized educations that are free from federal student loans. I do not think that a low-cost education would cause them to "be lazy" later in life; rather, much like launch aid for a company, it would give them a leg up in life that they would not normally have on reservations or in cities. However, it should not be mandatory and should be open to those American Indians who believe it to be a better option than remaining in the conditions under which they were born.

Land Development: I believe that Native American tribes should be given the same treatment as corporations when it comes to loans for land development from banks. These loans should be treated as tax-free until the land has been developed to a level equivalent to that of the land surrounding the reservation. This would hopefully encourage reservations to become more active in the marketplace and would improve property values, and thus living conditions, on reservations.

Sovereignty: I firmly believe that all Native Americans should be given dual citizenship, but to an extent that is not shared with any other nations. They should be treated as a sovereign people and should not be subject to any U.S. laws, with the exception of those established under treaties with their respective tribe(s). However, they should be given all the same rights as natural-born American citizens. I believe that this would encourage greater cooperation between tribes and state and federal governments. I also think that each Indian tribe should be given an embassy in Washington D.C. that can have a so-called Ambassador to the United States. These Ambassadors could then meet with Congress several times a year to discuss sovereignty relations and policy reform.

The current state of Native American affairs is one that has changed little since the Assimilation era of the 19th and early 20th Centuries. That no other racial group experiences the same level of discrimination from that time is astonishing and demands change. The issues I listed above more or less encompass the problems present on reservations and in cities. However, they are hardly a thorough representation of any issue. I believe that the solutions I listed above may be viable and logical ones, based on the research I have conducted both for this and previous projects. However, I am not guaranteeing their success. I can only hope that more people will learn more about this topic and contribute to the discussion of possible solutions. Native Americans must be included as equals in the conversation in order for solutions to hold any water. Only then can we reverse 530 years of racial tension and see each other as social, economic, and intellectual equals.

Bibliography

Aldrick, Philip. "Davos WEF 2011: Wealth inequality is the "most serious challenge for the world"." *The Telegraph*. Telegraph Media Group, 26 Jan. 2011. Web. 20 Nov. 2013. <http://www.telegraph.co.uk/finance/ financetopics/davos/8283310/Davos-WEF-2011-Wealth-inequality- is-the-most-serious-challenge-for-the-world.html>.

"American Indian/Alaska Native Profile."*The Office of Minority Health*. N.p., 17 Sept. 2012. Web. 16 Nov. 2013. <http://minorityhealth.hhs.gov/ templates/browse.aspx?lvl=2&lvlID=52>.

Anderson, Terry, and Dominic Parker. "Un-American Reservations | Hoover Institution." Defining Ideas. The Hoover Institution, 24 Feb. 2011. Web. 16 Nov. 2013<http://www.hoover.org/publications/defining- ideas/article/67756>.

"Cherokee Nation v. Georgia - 30 U.S. 1 (1831)." *Justia US Supreme Court Center.* N.p., n.d. Web. 16 Nov. 2013. <https://supreme.justia.com/cases/federal/us/30/1/case.html>.

"Combating Racism in Australia A discussion paper by HREOC for the World Conference Against Racism." *Australian Human Rights Commission.* N.p., n.d. Web. 8 Dec. 2013. <http://www.humanrights.gov.au/hreoc-website-racial-discrimination-national-consultations- racism-and>.

"Commercial bank branches (per 100,000 adults)." *The World Bank.* N.p., n.d. Web. 14 Nov.b2013. <http://data.worldbank.org/indicator/FB.CBK. BRCH.P5?order=wbapi_data_value_2011+wb api_data_value+wbapi_ data_value-last&sort=asc>.

"Commercial Banks in the U.S. (USNUM)." - *FRED.* N.p., 8 Nov. 2013. Web. 20 Nov. 2013. <http://research.stlouisfed.org/fred2/series/USNUM>.

"Educational Attainment: 2000." *United States Census.* N.p., n.d. Web. 14 Nov. 2013. <http://www.census.gov/prod/2003pubs/c2kbr-24.pdf>.

"Eric Holder Outlining New Justice Department Drug Sentencing Reforms."*Community TV* 1. N.p., 12 Aug. 2013. Web. 20 Nov. 2013. <http://communitytv1.com/web/index.php/tech-blog/item/214-eric-holder-outlining-new-justice-department-drug-sentencing-reforms>.

"FFIEC Median Family Income Listing,"*FFIEC.* N.p., 1 July 2013. Web. 20 Nov. 2013. <http://www.ffiec.gov/hmda/Medianincome. htm#MSAincome>.

"Forbes 400." *Forbes.* Forbes Magazine, n.d. Web. 20 Nov. 2013. <http://www.forbes.com/forbes- 400/list/>.

Frazer, R. W. *A Literary History of India.* New York: Haskell House, 1970. Print.

Hargreaves, Steve. "Poverty rate 15%, median income $51,017." *CNNMoney.* Cable News Network, 17 Sept. 2013. Web. 20 Nov. 2013. <http://money.cnn.com/2013/09/17/news/economy/poverty- income/>.

"How Many Americans Have There Been?." *A Niche in the Library of Babel.* N.p., 19 Jan. 2010. Web. 20 Nov. 2013. <http://babelniche.wordpress. com/2010/01/19/how-many-americans-have-there-been/>.

Huisenga, Sarah. "Newt Gingrich: Poor kids don't work "unless it's illegal"."*CBSNews.* CBS Interactive, 1 Dec. 2011. Web. 20 Nov. 2013. <http://www.cbsnews.com/news/newt-gingrich-poor-kids-dont-work-unless-its-illegal/>.

Hunt, Billie, and Charles Harrington. "The Impending Educational Crisis for American Indians: Higher Education at the Crossroads." *Journal of Multicultural, Gender, and Minority Studies* 2.2 (2008): 1-11. Scientific Journals International. Web. 15 Nov. 2013.

"Inflation Calculator: Bureau of Labor Statistics." *U.S. Bureau of Labor Statistics*. U.S. Bureau of Labor Statistics, n.d. Web. 16 Nov. 2013. <http://www.bls.gov/data/inflation_calculator.htm>.

Koppisch, John. "Why Are Indian Reservations So Poor? A Look At The Bottom 1%." *Forbes*. Forbes Magazine, 13 Dec. 2011. Web. 24 Nov. 2013. <http://www.forbes.com/sites/johnkoppisch/2011/12/13/why-are-indian-reservations-so-poor-a-look- at-the-bottom-1/>.

"Life Expectancy at Birth." *WHO | World Health Organization*. N.p., n.d. Web. 14 Nov. 2013. <http://gamapserver.who.int/gho/interactive_charts/mbd/life_expectancy/atlas.html>.

Miller, Jake. "Obama nominates Native American woman to federal bench."*CBSNews*. CBS Interactive, 20 Sept. 2013. Web. 20 Nov. 2013. <http://www.cbsnews.com/8301-250_162-57603968/>.

"Minorities and Homelessness." *National Coalition for the Homeless*. National Coalition for the Homeless, n.d. Web. 20 Nov. 2013. <http://www.nationalhomeless.org/factsheets/minorities.html>.

"Natives top violent crime list again."*Indianz.com*. N.p., 8 Apr. 2002. Web. 20 Nov. 2013. <http://www.indianz.com/News/show.asp?ID=law02/04082002-1>.

"Oglala Lakota College Case Statement."*Oglala Lakota College*. N.p., 29 Feb. 2012. Web. 14 Nov. 2013. <http://webcache.googleusercontent.com/search?q=cache:BnC5ts127joJ:www.olc.edu/~jdudek/webfolder/task-force/case2.29.doc+&cd=4&hl=en&ct=clnk&gl=us>.

"One in 10 hate crimes target American Indians." *Indianz.com*. N.p., 1 Oct. 2001. Web. 20 Nov. 2013. <http://www.indianz.com/News/show.asp?ID=law/1012001-5>.

Pickering, Kathleen, and David Mushinski. "ACCESS TO CREDIT ON THE PINE RIDGE INDIAN RESERVATION:BANKS, ALTERNATIVE SOURCES OF CREDIT, AND THE LAKOTA FUND." *Lakota Funds*. N.p., n.d. Web. 14 Nov. 2013. <http://lakotafunds.org/docs/access.pdf>.

"Pine Ridge Indian Reservation: Population and Housing." *South Dakota Tribal Relations*. N.p., n.d. Web. 14 Nov. 2013. <http://www.sdtribalrelations.com/new/tribalstatprofiles/oststatprofile2011.pdf>.

"Prevalence of overweight, obesity and extreme obesity among adults: United States, trends 1960-62 through 2005-2006 ." *Centers for Disease Control and Prevention*. Centers for Disease Control and Prevention, 23 Dec. 2009. Web. 14 Nov. 2013. <http://www.cdc.gov/nchs/data/hestat/overweight/overweight_adult.htm>.

Robertson, Dwanna. "The Myth of Indian Casino Riches - ICTMN.com." *Indian Country Today Media Network.com*. N.p., 23 June 2012. Web. 8 Dec. 2013. <http://indiancountrytodaymedianetwork.com/2012/06/23/myth-indian-casino-riches>.

Robertson, Lindsay. "Native Americans and the Law: Native Americans Under Current United States Law." *Native Americans and the Law : Native Americans Under Current United States Law*. The University of Oklahoma Law Center, n.d. Web. 16 Nov. 2013. <http://thorpe.ou.edu/guide/robertson.html>.

"Shannon County QuickFacts from the US Census Bureau." *State and County Quickfacts*. United States Census, 27 June 2013. Web. 14 Nov. 2013. <http://quickfacts.census.gov/qfd/states/46/46113.html>.

Smith, Nathaniel. *The Chinese Exclusion Era: Conflict and Compromise on Gold Mountain*. 2008. Film. http://www.youtube.com/watch?v=oCY3s6D7aF0

Strauss, Valerie. "Five stereotypes about poor families and education." *The Answer Sheet*. The Washington Post, 28 Oct. 2013. Web. 20 Nov. 2013. <http://www.washingtonpost.com/blogs/answer- sheet/wp/2013/10/28/five-stereotypes-about-poor-families-and-education/>.

"The State of the Native Nations:Conditions Under U.S. Policies of Self-Determination." *The Harvard Project on American Indian Economic Development*. Oxford University Press, n.d. Web. 20 Nov. 2013. <http://isites.harvard.edu/fs/docs/icb.topic177572.files/SONN_Final_01_09_07.pdf>.

"The Wealthiest Americans Ever." *The New York Times*. N.p., 15 July 2007. Web. 20 Nov. 2013. <http://www.nytimes.com/ref/business/20070715_GILDED_GRAPHIC.html>.

Thomas, William. "What Is Objectivism?."*The Atlas Society*. N.p., n.d. Web. 25 Nov. 2013. <http://www.atlassociety.org/what_is_objectivism>.

Williams, Timothy . "Quietly, Indians Reshape Cities and Reservations." *The New York Times*. N.p., 13 Apr. 2013. Web. 10 Oct. 2013. <http://www.nytimes.com/2013/04/14/us/as-american-indians-move-to-cities-old-and-new-challenges-follow.html?_r=0>.

∎ Zoot Suit

By Xochitl Villezcas

Xochitl Villezcas' research paper begins with a narrative that represents the experience of Mexican and Mexican Americans during the Zoot Suit Riots of the 1940s. It is a powerful depiction of a clash between cultures in which one is misunderstood as they seek to develop and maintain their identity through their clothing. Villezcas' depth of research explores the changes in clothing style from the riots up to present day while addressing both the cultural and socio-economic positions each generation has found themselves situated in. Through this in-depth look, Villezcas navigates the conflicted spaces that develop between ethnic heritage and community and the dominant culture.

The Result of the Zoot Suit Riots

My name is Panjilo Ramirez and this makes me an automatic target. It is the end of June 1943 and things are just getting worse. I live in Los Angeles, California in the common neighborhood. When the sun sets I like to get ready to take my ruca out. It's Saturday night and we want to have a good time in the city. We do not have a lot of money but we live well.

I begin to get ready. I like to have my pants that are called Drapes nice and ironed. They are long and go above my waist. They are loose at the top and tight at the bottom. These pants are meant for dancing. I told you we like to have a good time. My shirt is called a Lisa. Mine is white and a button up. Believe me you should have that ironed too. Nicely tucked in and buttoned up with the last two top buttons undone. Your pants need a little help staying up, you know, that's why we have suspenders. Now you have your cadena, place one end of the chain hook it to one of the front loops of the pants and place the other end to your wallet and place in in the back pocket. Now I can 't say I lost my wallet when we are out. Stacy Adams shoes. Nice and shiny. Keep them that way. Finally the coat, nicely slide it on and let it hang. This coat is long, it's supposed to be. Lastly, you can't forget the hat. I am ready to go out. I hope my ruca is looking as good.

I get into my car and drive down the street to pick up my girl. I cannot get over how amazing she always looks. She has her knee high skirt going with the long coat and her black heels. Her hair is perfect and so is she. We walk to my car and I opened the door for her. I had the night all planned out for us. We were going to eat at this nice restaurant that we all hang out around, then take her to the movie; I know she likes that. Things have been going crazy around this time so I carry a bat in my car just in case. I have to take care of my girl, you know?

We are cruising, making our way to the downtown area. We see a lot of the vatos on our way there and we wave at them. I am thinking about what I want to eat. This restaurant has so much good food. I am still talking to my ruca, she seems very excited. She hasn't gone out in some time. She asks me what we are doing tonight and well I told her it was a surprise. However, she kept insisting. I could not resist that beautiful face, so I told her. She was happy that we were going to the movies. She heard about one of the movies that her friend went and saw and she wanted to watch it. I was happy she was excited.

*I looked in the review mirror and I realized that the same car had been following me for some time. I pay more attention to the driver and the passengers. They look like sailors (**view Figure 1**). Why are they following us? We have done nothing wrong. My girl notices my change in expression. She asks me what's wrong. I told her a group of sailors is following us. We reached our destination and I park. I get out of the car and I told her not to get out of the car. She told me not to fight it. I could see the worried look on her face. We've had friends that have also been stopped and the result is not good. The car from behind pulled up next to me and the guys came out. Some with bats. I asked them what their problem was and why they are following us. They didn't even respond. A couple came towards me and grabbed me.*

I felt the punches in the head. Kicks at my ribs. Tossed to one side to another. I wished and hope she stayed in the car. I was losing what I was thinking. I could feel every blow. I no longer knew how many were there. My coat came off They yanked one shoe off followed by my pants. I don't remember when my shirt was pulled off I felt something warm running down my face and it was not water. I covered my face as much as I could.

I heard her screams. Why didn't she grab my bat? I wished they wouldn't harm her. Come on who would hit a girl? !felt cold. Was I naked? Please diosito keep her safe. I see the lights of safety. Red, white and blue. But they weren't. The blows stopped. I was being lifted up and arrested. Author's note: inspired by the movie *American Me.*

What initiated the Chicano Movement during the I 960's was looking at who were the heroes of "back then" (Licon). When we talk about the heroes of the movement's beginning, one would think of Zapata, Pancho Villa, and the Pachucos. Looking back upon the Pachucos in the 1940's, first known as the zootsuiters, they were Mexican and Mexican American youth and adults. A lot of these youth were first generation immigrant children. Many at this time, the youth, were fighting an issue of culture liminality. To their parents these youth were too Americanized and to the Americans they were too Mexican. Wearing the zoot suit was a way to rebel against society, to show society that they were a different person. However, there was an issue with authorities on a "Mexican crime wave" that was believed and put upon every Mexican American. Sailors, servicemen, and civilians took issues into their own hands to fight against anyone wearing a zoot suit. The attire of the zoot suit was initiated and formed around the Jazz era. The zoot suiters influenced culture identification at the time and later generations with similar style and the transformation to today's *cholo* style. Women also have had an important role: they challenged gender identification and the societal norms through the zoot suit attire. Zoot suiters also influenced media during the era and many musical artists today have co-opted the zoot suit for their publicity.

The zoot suiters were predominantly worn by members of the Mexican and Mexican American communities. They were also worn by working class whites and African Americans. However for the purpose of this research I will be focusing on the Mexicans and Mexican Americans communities that wore the zoot suits. Zootsuiters was a style that Mexican and Mexican American encountered from the African American era during

World War II. However, zootsuiters transformed it to their own style. It was also known as *El tacuche*, (**view Figure 2**). The suit brought upon a sense of empowerment to oneself against a society that was against them. It was a way that "powerless populations craft their own identities and claim dignity" (Alvarez). They were rebelling against this liminality that was put upon them from both societies. There were some gang that used the zoot suit and after that the others were automatically seen as gang members. However, these people were targeted as unpatriotic and un American (Alvarez). The Zoot Suit Riots had begun after the many clashes with sailors and servicemen with the zootsuiters.

In the late 1930's and the early 1940's during the wave of first generation Mexican Americans that wore the zoot suits there was a "Mexican crime wave" that was created by the police, according to the discussion with Dr. Licon. People, specifically Mexicans and Mexican Americans would be arrested for having little things such as bats and tire irons in their cars. In 1942, a man, Jose Diaz, was killed in a gang fight in the Sleepy Lagoon are in South Los Angeles: "Hundreds of innocent young men and women from central and eastern Los Angeles were rounded up during this period, fingerprinted, and booked ... to reassure the white middle class that wartime police force was indeed capable of maintaining law" (Pagan). According to Dr. Licon, about five to six hundred Mexican American youth were arrested to show that the police were cracking down this violence after the murder: "Despite a lack of evidence, twenty two individuals between ages of seventeen and twenty-four ... were arrested, charged with murder and assault, and tried" (Alvarez 45). There were also women that were tried. There were "two of the indicated youths [that] asked for a separate trial and were subsequently released" (Meier 191). These two men had used lawyers whereas the other twenty-two men had to use the public offense attorney and were tried. The men weren't allowed to change their clothes or cut their hair and were not allowed to consult with their attorneys. All this was going against their constitutional rights (Alvarez). When prosecuted the way they were dressed reaffirmed how guilty they were because of how they looked. On the other hand, the women weren't given a trial. Dr. Jimmy Patino, a historian and an assistant professor at the University of Minnesota in the Department of Chicano and Chicana Studies, talks about these young women, girls that were in there teens were treated unfair. He continues to say that these girls were taken from their parents and became wards of the state. They were placed "in the Ventura School for Girls, a notorious reform school, until they turned twenty-one" (Alvarez 45). For the way that these mostly youths were dressed they were automatically seen as delinquents.

The Zoot Suit Riots began in Los Angeles, 1943 after the Sleepy Lagoon case. There were still constant racial attacks against Mexicans and Mexican Americans. During this time the United States was in World War II. Many Mexicans were still coming to the United States to help with the work force. The year before, 1942, it was the beginning of the relocation of the Japanese, while other German and Italian American people at the time were not relocated themselves (Chacon and Davis). When the violence against the Japanese lowered, "the brunt of wartime racial prejudice and mob or vigilante violence, especially in the Los Angeles area, was directed against Chicanos and African-American youth" (Chacon and Davis). Many that were targeted were those that wore the zoot suit.

The Mexican and Mexican American youth wore zoot suits and the youth were also known as *Pachucos*. This attire "had been conflated with a racialized and almost entirely imaginary menace of teenage gangsters and draft dodgers" (Chacon and Davis). Signifying that the people who wore this attire were seen as troubled and trying to avoid being drafted to the war. In fact, "Mexican Americans [had] joined the armed forces to help defend U.S. democracy in Europe, the Pacific, and elsewhere ... more than 350,000 served in the armed forces during World War II" (Alvarez 17). The Zoot Suit Riots began after the navy servicemen had said that they were attacked by the zoot suiters. Many service men and marines went out to look for these Mexican zootsuiters. Every single person that wore one that they found was beaten and stripped down to their underwear **(view Figure 3)**. Many other minorities were also targeted. They were "all violently pulled off trolleys and beaten, some as young as 12" (Reft), **(view Figure 4)**. The police did not do anything but "cleaned-up" after the service men by arresting anyone wearing a zoot suit that they had encountered. There were also many Mexican Americans that not only served in the war but also wore the zoot suit and fought alongside the zoot suiters.

The attire of the zoot suit was worn in favor of what the fashion was: "Mexican Americans turned towards zoot suit culture as they struggled to define themselves" (Heiler). However, during this wartime era "zoot suiters were usually construed as antiwar, unpatriotic, and even pro-Axis [and] they were regularly being drafted or were voluntarily joining the navy and army" (Alvarez 196). It is said as the Zoot Suit Riots subsided and men were returning home from the war they and the youth started to change the way they began to dress. The youth were still in constant state of culture liminality. They wanted to fit in to this wartime country. They wanted to be seen as more patriotic. Therefore slowly they transformed to wearing ironed khakis pants and a tucked in white tee (Licon). This attire was meant to resemble the way that the servicemen were dressed. One has to remember that these communities were still looked down upon.

Today the culture identification has changed that is now called the *cholo* style, a gangster look, which older generations still wear. This consists of ironed pants, usually khakis or black Dickies, with a white tucked in tee and a flannel shirt button up just at the top or a very loose button up shirt also button only at the top **(view Figure 5)**. In an interview with ex-gang ·members from El Paso, Texas I asked what was it like to wear or how it felt to wear the style *cholo* style. They responded, "It was pride, it was representing the neighborhood. You would get respect." The reasons of wearing this style still resemble the same reasons that the zoot suiter had. They talked about how this style in their neighborhood was a norm everybody dressed the same. For the reason that the outfit was affordable. They would get bullied if they weren't wearing the style. Later in the interview, they mentioned that wearing the *cholo* style in the 80's was to just be dressed nicely. It was a way to show that people of color had something even though they came out of poverty.

The women zootsuiters were among dressed similarly as the men. It was seen as the "in style" at the time. Many Mexican American women youth wanted to wear the style, causing them to save their money in order to purchase the attire. It was "their own style of dress, consisting of a long finger-tip coat or letterman's sweater, draped slacks or a short, full skirt above or just to their brown knees, high bobby socks and huaraches" (Ramirez 56). They were accused of being masculine because they also wore a zoot suit similar to the men (**view Figure 6**). However, they wore dark lip-stick and heavy mascara, with a high bouffant. It was said by many Anglo Americans that the women would hide knives in their hair because of how high it was (Ramirez). A woman in the book *The Women in the Zoot Suit* by Catherine Ramirez explained that she didn't understand how a knife could fit in the hair.

Women zootsuiters' identity during the 1940's are described differently, depending on who one asks. First for many Anglo Americans, women zoot suiters were often seen as negatively as the men. During this time period, many people were still accustomed to seeing women look feminine with long skirts and attending the home. However, it changed when women went into the work force, yet still having a feminine side. While women zoot suiters were also looked as unpatriotic for the unnecessary fabric they were using, they were also targeted for "unbridled female sexuality [and] juvenile delinquency" (Ramirez 69). Women wanted to be viewed as patriotic if they had a feminine charm and having daintiness. On the other hand, women zootsuiters were seen as "wild, dirty, and unkempt in the Anglo press" (Ramirez 71). Thus, expressing that women zootsuiters were no good to society. Not only Anglos targeted women zootsuiters but also the parents. Many of the women zootsuiters were second generation Mexican Americans. The parents thought of the zootsuiter style to be a bad influence on their female children (Ramirez).

Women zootsuiters were seen as too masculine for society. They wore similar clothes as the men did. This was a way that they were going against gender norms during World War II. Women were not supposed to be wearing clothing that looked masculine unless when they were in the work force. In fact, "women who crossed-dressed in public or failed to wear at least three articles of women's clothing could be arrested for 'male impersonation'" (Ramirez 79). Women zootsuiters can easily identifiable as women because of their make-up and hair. However, it is argued that just because they were wearing men clothing, they weren't directly seen as women. Thus, being easily identified as men and seen as unpatriotic because the women "weren't" helping the Homefront. Going against gender norms for women can also be seen as being rebellion at the time but it was a form of resistance that women had during the 1940's in the larger American society. Women showed "that masculinity was not the sole property of men" (Alvarez 82). Wearing the zoot suit for women was not something they did because they were in a gang, many did not take part in such thing, but because they were taking part in the style that was going on. The style was form to identify oneself and a form of resistance against the normal society expectation.

The influence of the women zootsuiters in today's *cholas*, Latina gangster look, has had similar impact of showing resistance. In a discussion session at the National Association for Chicana and Chicano Studies conference (NACCS) three women talked about "The Culture of Resistance." They spoke about the way Pachucas, women zoot suiters dressed and their make-up was a form that is still used in today's *cholas*. They described that the cholas of today to also fight against gender norms. They were the same clothes as men and are seen to be as tough as them **(view Figure 7)**. Although the women zootsuiters weren't exactly in gangs, most of the women that wear the *chola* style aren't as well. These women are constantly "looking behind their backs," for trouble that may come. The women continued to talk about the way that their make-up resembles how tough they had to look, whether they were with their "man" or going out with some friends. Society still places an image for what women should look like and as the Pachucas did, the cholas are also going against the way that society would want to place them.

People use the zoot suit attire in different forms of media to gain publicity. However, certain people use the style in a form of appreciation it or a form of appropriating it. During the era of the zoot suits, there was an actor German Valdes that was known as Tin Tan **(view Figure 8)**. He became a comedian known for wearing the zoot suit attire. He made his way through Ciudad Juarez, Chihuahua, Mexico and throughout the United States. To "Mexican audiences [they] saw Tin Tan as a victim of Anglo-American assimilation" (Mazon 5). Explained by Dr. Licon, German Valdes was someone who previously wore the zoot suit. Although Valdes was using the zoot suit attire as his stage costume and used it in his comedies: he understood what it was meant to him and others. Therefore even if he was seen to be assimilated he appreciated the zoot suit.

Now there are many musical artists that are using specifically the women zootsuiters and the current *chola* style to gain some publicity. In the conversation with the three women at NACCS they touched a little on this subject. They gave the musical artist Rihanna that have used the *chota* style for Halloween costume and was a form of appropriating the *chola* look. For the reason that she doesn't understand where it came from. "[Rihanna] describes herself as a '*chola*' ... [referring] to a Mexican-American subculture with roots in the Pachuco and zoot-suit traditions in California" (Reporter). The three women continue explain why Rihanna and other artists are appropriating the look with a video called, "Cholas Talk ... Fashion." In this video there are series of *cholas* are examining what these artists are wearing. They describe them to be wearing the whole thing wrong and doesn't give them the "stamp of approval." The women are dressed as cholas and understand the meaning of wearing the style.

Wearing a zoot suit was a way for people, especially Mexican Americans, to shape an identity that corresponded to themselves. In many ways the zoot suit was a way these men and women were able to be who they wanted in a society that was racially discriminatory. They would be attack and harassed by those that were serving the country overseas against racism. It is very ironic that servicemen were fighting the opposite issue in the United States. Zoot suiters stood up for themselves and continuing to wear the zoot suit even after they were threatened showed the empowerment that they had. The men and women had saved a lot of their earnings to pay for a zoot suit. They felt proud, respected and powerful when wearing the attire. These feelings are still felt in our culture today. The *cholo* and *chola* style represents a way empowerment in their communities. It is a tough look that gives a sense of power to these communities that are powerless. The feeling of racism and oppression are still ongoing and gives reasons for these communities to show in material things what they work so hard for to not be looked down upon.

The zoot suit attire has come a long way from the 1940's. Even though it is not a common fashion today as it once was, the transition of the style still remains in Mexican American communities. The attire of the zoot suit is still used today for special occasions in the Latino community. As part of the Latino community, people use it in family reunions, weddings, funerals, quinceafieras, sweet 15, or any other party because it is part of their identity from the past. As the transition from the zoot suit to the ironed khakis and white tee's to the *cholo* style and everything in between the style is passed on finding its own cultural identification among youth. Media has always portrayed the young zoot suiters and cholo to be associated with violence and gangs. Nonetheless it is just a style that Mexican Americans have used to find a place that they could fit in. Culture liminality in the United States is still common amongst many and through the clothing people wear helps distinguish themselves as different from the dominant culture.

Figures

Figure 1: Servicemen riding around on a car during the Zoot Suit Riots. *American Experience*. June 1943. Web. 03 May 2016.

Figure 2: The Zoot Suit attire and what everything is called. *Zoot Suit Discovery Guide*. 2016. Web. 03 May 2016.

Figure 3: Zootsuiters beaten and stripped of their clothing. Teenage Film. June 1943. Web. 03 May 2016.

Figure 4: Zoot Suit Riots. Credit AP Images.

Figure 5: Jose Villezcas dressed for a sua *Author's photograph*. 05 March 2016.

Figure 6: Woman zootsuiter dressed to go out, Los Angeles Public Library. A Group of 7 women zootsuiters posing for a photo, Los Angeles Public Library.

Figure 7: Women dressed in the variety of the chola style. Photo by Kate Moross, www.flickr.com/photos/katemo/5082852013.

Figure 8: Tin Tan in his comedies. *Mexico Unmasked*. August 2011 Web. 03 May 2016.

Works Cited

Alvarez, Luis. *The Power of the Zoot: Youth Culture and Resistance during World War II*. Berkeley: U of California, 2008. Print.

American Me. Dir. Edward James Olmos. Prod. Edward James Olmos. By Floyd Mutrux and Desmond Nakano. Perf. Edward James Olmos and Pepe Serna. Universal Pictures, 1992.

Chacon, Justin Akers, and Mike Davis. *No One Is Illegal: Fighting Violence and State Repression on the U.S-Mexico Border*. Chicago, IL: Haymarket, 2006. Print.

Hailer, Charles. "Zoot Suit Riot." *Teenage*. 24 Mar. 2014. Web. 25 Apr. 2016.

Licon, Gerardo. "Mexican American ZootSuiters in El Paso Texas: Pachucos, Tirilis and Kalifas." Chicano and Latino Studies. Scott Hall Room 2, Minneapolis. 25 Mar. 2016. Lecture.

Mazon, Mauricio. The Zoot-suit Riots: *The Psychology of Symbolic Annihilation*. Austin: U of Texas, 1984. Print.

Meier, Matt S., and Feliciano Ribera. The Chicanos: A History of Mexican Americans. New York: Hill and Wang, 1972. 191-196. Print.

Meyer, Agnes E. "Zoot-Suiters-- A New Youth Movement." *The Washington Post* (1923-1954):2. Jun 13 1943. ProQuest. Web. 10 Apr. 2016.

Pagan, Eduardo Obregon. *Murder at the Sleepy Lagoon: Zoot Suits, Race, and Riot in Wartime L.A*. Chapel Hill: U ofNorth Carolina, 2003. Print.

Patifio, Jimmy. Personal Interview. 19 Apr. 2016.

Ramirez, Catherine Sue. *The Woman in the Zoot Suit: Gender, Nationalism, and the Cultural Politics of Memory*. Durham: Duke UP, 2009. 64-82. Print

Reft, Ryan. "Seventy Years Later: The Zoot Suit Riots and the Complexity of Youth Culture." KCET. KCETLink, 30 May 2013 . Web. 27 Feb. 2016.

Reporter, Daily Mail. "Copycat! Rihanna Dresses as a Latina Gangster for Halloween Two Days after Chris Brown's Girlfriend Karreuche Tran Wears Almost Identical Costume." *Mail Online*. Associated Newspapers, 02 Nov. 2013. Web. 20 Apr. 2016.

Soriano, Lucecita, Maria Camacho, and Ana Scarlett Celis. "Pachucas & Cholas: A Culture of Resistance." National Association for Chicana and Chicano Studies. Denver, Colorado. 07 Apr. 2016. Lecture.

Villezcas, Jose. Darlina Ponce, Rudy Cordova. Personal Interview. 22 Apr. 2016.

Information About Writing Studies Undergraduate

B.S. in Technical Writing and Communication (TWC) -50 credits

Technical Writing and Communication (TWC) involves communicating complex information to specific audiences with clarity and accuracy. Technical communicators write, organize, edit, and design information for a variety of workplace settings in business, health, technology, science, environment, and law. Turn your love of writing into a professional career with a TWC major.

As a technical writing student, you will study theories of rhetoric and communication and apply principles of audience analysis, digital writing, editing, information design, and usability. In our courses, you will engage in writing as a process and examine writing within diverse cultures and communities and develop real-world, marketable skills.

What are the top 5 reasons to major in TWC?

1. Be that unique person who understands technical or scientific information and can clearly explain it!
2. Join a career area predicted to grow by 15% over the next decade—technical communication.
3. Practice using the latest digital writing technologies; plus free access to Lynda.com.
4. Network with alumni about real-world writing and new job opportunities.
5. Impress your friends and colleagues with knowledge about Aristotle and ancient rhetoric.

TWC majors take 35 credits of Writing Studies courses (WRIT) and 15 credits from one of four sub-plans areas. Your sub-plan allows you to focus on an area of interest by taking courses from outside the department to fulfill your degree requirements.

TWC Sub-plans

1. 1. **Information Technology and Design**: This sub-plan offers courses in web design, media production, information technology, visual rhetoric, and message design. If you have a background or interest in computer science, engineering, design, visual communication, or technology, you may find this a useful emphasis area.
2. **Biological and Health Sciences:** This sub-plan offers courses in medical writing or communication related to public health, pharmacy, or biomedical technology. If you have a background or interest in biology, chemistry, anatomy, public health, nursing, or medicine, you may find this a useful emphasis area.
3. **Legal Discourse and Public Policy:** This sub-plan offers courses in government, politics, law, and public policy. If you have a background or interest in political science, economics, sociology, law, or philosophy, you may find this a useful emphasis area.
4. **Environmental Science**: This sub-plan offers courses in natural resources, sustainability, land conservation, and environmental issues. If you have a background or interest in environmental studies, geography, ecology, applied economics, forestry and natural resources, urban studies, and earth sciences, you may find this a useful emphasis area.

Minor in Technical Writing and Communication (TWC)-16 credits

The TWC minor enhances your degree program with professional writing and communication skills. These skills can be transferred to careers in a wide range of fields, including today's fast-growing science and technology industries.

Courses in this minor especially focus on Writing Studies (WRIT) courses (10 credits) that build your skills in professional writing, editing, and presentation or visual display design. In addition, minor students can also choose to develop additional technical communication specialties through two upper-division WRIT elective courses (6 credits) such as public writing, writing with digital technologies, intersections of TWC and the law, and many more.

For more information about Technical Writing and Communication programs or classes, contact Barb Horvath (horva003@umn or 612-624-1902) or visit www.cla.umn.edu/writing-studies.